MAGIC MOUNTAINS

MAGIC MOUNTAINS

RENNIE McOWAN

MAINSTREAM
PUBLISHING
EDINBURGH AND LONDON

First published in Great Britain in 1996 by
MAINSTREAM PUBLISHING COMPANY (EDINBURGH) LTD
7 Albany Street
Edinburgh EH1 3UG

ISBN 1 85158 707 1

A catalogue record for this book is available from the British Library

Typeset in Adobe Garamond by Litho Link Ltd, Welshpool, Powys, Wales
Printed and bound in Great Britain by Butler & Tanner Ltd, Frome

For Liz Patterson

Mountaineer, Gaelic enthusiast, Highland historian, descendant of the Stewarts of Appin and Atholl, and good friend. Without her help this book would not have been written.

CONTENTS

ACKNOWLEDGEMENTS

I would like to thank the Scottish Arts Council for a travel grant which enabled me to complete the researches for this book.

I also want to express my gratitude to many good friends, contacts and outdoor companions who helped provide information, anecdotes or undertook pieces of research or who joined in expeditions. They include Captain Ronnie Leask, Sandy Williamson, Paul Van Vlissingen, Caroline Tisdall, Frank Tucker, Willie Thom, Peter Meech, Liz Robinson, Màiri MacDonald, Dr Elaine Petrie, Nigel Hawkins, Anne-Marie Boyle, Maurice Fleming, John Mitchell, Libby Urquhart, Chris Lowell, plus many others – some of whom are mentioned by name in the following pages. Two dear friends who contributed a great deal, John Rundle and Alastair McGowan, died in recent years.

Special thanks are due to my patient family, my wife, Agnes, and children, Lesley, Michael, Tom and Niall, and to my good friend, Isobel Quinn, who put up with my handwriting and often untidy typing and processor material and produced an acceptable manuscript. All mistakes are my own.

THE FEY PLACES

When a feeling of deep foreboding, of a sense of evil, of oppressiveness, of bad vibes, strikes two people *separately* in the same place then one has to ponder why.

Many years ago my wife (to be) and I had a hillwalking holiday on the lovely Argyllshire islands of Islay and Jura. We hired a boat to take us from Port Askaig on Islay across to Jura so that we could climb the Paps – the three breast-shaped mountains which catch the eye in so many views to the west. It was in the days before the daily ferry ran on that route.

The Paps are marvellous hills with wide views over the western seaboard and inland. They can also be a gruelling trek with steep, stony sections. We abandoned the third Pap – but have since returned from the eastern side – and made our way over rough moorland to the western coast. We found we were slightly tight for time to pick up the boat again and took a direct line along the coast on undulating moorland. It was rough going. At one point we descended into a little hollow where a burn came across the moor. It fell in a little *eas* or waterfall into a small pool and the sides were green and shaded.

I was slightly ahead of Agnes and stopped on the lip. She caught up with me and I was just about to suggest a halt when I found myself dropping down into the hollow. I looked around. There was nothing markedly special about it. The mild wind set the heather fringes quivering on the top of the banks, the little burn gurgled into its clear pool, the murmur of the sea was just to our right. But I found it so oppressive that it made me uneasy and, without saying anything, I hopped the burn and leaped up the other side.

Agnes joined me and we set off across the moor. After a bit I said, 'I was going to suggest we stop at that burn, but the place made me uneasy.

Daft, isn't it? It must have felt close being out of the wind.'

Agnes looked at me for a minute and replied, 'That's odd, I felt exactly the same thing, but I didn't want to say anything in case I sounded silly or I was imagining things.

'But it *was* eerie. I was all for sitting down and then I said to myself "I don't like this place". I was about to call to you to stop, but you were already clambering up the bank and then I didn't want to remain there. It did feel frightening.'

We discussed this for a moment or two and temporarily agreed to put it down to the fact that it was a shaded hollow, but it has stuck in our minds over many years.

I did spend some time trying to find out whether any dark deed had happened near there, but without success. Witches are reputed to haunt the nearby Paps and the Gulf of Corrievreckan far to the north and a belief in faeries was common in past times, but all that was in the realm of general lore.

However, it did act like a kind of trigger which set me speculating as to why some outdoor folk – balanced, intelligent people of integrity – have 'seen' ghosts, wraiths, spectres, bogles and faeries in our hills, moors, glens and straths, and why so many bothies apparently have very noisy spectral beings, including poltergeists, banging on walls, shoving furniture around and stamping on the floorboards. Hillwalkers have sensed 'invisible people' being with them or of 'life' in empty corners.

Other than our mysterious hollow on Jura and an alleged ghost (heard, not seen) in a Highland cottage, I have never personally experienced such happenings. I do believe our hollow was fey in some fashion. But I accept that other people have had inexplicable experiences and that they are credible witnesses.

It is not a matter for dismissive levity. It is a serious part of the history of our hills and applies to all Scotland, not just the Highlands. Its roots lie deep in Scottish culture and folklore. I firmly believe that these mysterious experiences, including psychic incidents, reported in modern times have their roots in the cultures of the past and with the lives of our predecessors as hill people. It is an on-going story and the last chapters may well be written in our own times.

That wonderful naturalist, Sir Frank Fraser Darling, who died in 1979

– an ecologist of world stature whose researches into red deer are particularly remembered and who was a scourge of the establishment of his day – wrote:

> At the back of everything I get a sense of great age, dark things done and secrets held. This sense of the feel of places is queer. It hardly bears description in a gathering of intelligent people, but it cannot be disregarded in the Highlands. Explanation should be sought along physical or psychological lines, but the psychological result is there to be contended with and cannot be escaped.

Some Celtic scholars think that many people perhaps had an extra dimension to them in past times which dwindled and has almost become lost. It enabled them to 'see' people and events which others could not. Some children still have this capacity from time to time and instances of claimed second sight do linger on.

An old friend, Affleck Gray, of Pitlochry, retired landscape design consultant, historian and author of *The Big Grey Man of Ben MacDhui*, has a lifetime's experience of the hills and of researching legends in the Cairngorms. He says:

> Yes, I do believe people long ago had an extra dimension to their faculties and it was all very real to them. I don't know if they ever 'saw' anything in the normal sense. It was an acute awareness which we don't have, like the senses of a dog. They were more aware of things than we are. I think some people still have the same senses as in the old days. It was quite common and not confined to the Highlands.

I once discussed much of this subject at length with Sydney Scroggie, the blind and disabled mountaineer, as part of a BBC programme. Syd had a leg blown off and was blinded by a mine when serving with the Lovat Scouts in Italy during the Second World War. He still returns to his beloved hills, stumping along on a tin leg and holding on to a strap from the rucksack of the person in front. He was a widely experienced mountaineer before he was so seriously wounded and has a highly developed sense of intuition and perception. Syd wrote:

I have discovered that it is not the visual side of things in the hills that constitutes the profoundest aspect of the experience, any more than it is the croak of the ptarmigan, the scent of the heather, the feel of granite under your fingers or any other of the merely physical phenomena which are part and parcel of the hills.

What draws you there is an inner experience; something psychological, something poetic, which perhaps cannot be fully understood when the physical aspect of things gets in the way when you can see.

The older generations claimed they 'saw' beings which we now call faeries, banshees or witches, and our hill names make this clear.

The second most powerful strand in the links between ancient and modern is in the differing methods of interpreting landscape. On one hand, there exists an attitude of folklore – of personal association, of the soul and spirit; of something which *lived.* On the other: scientific, clinical, impersonal, unemotional, technical.

To the hill people of the past, Highland or Lowland, the land was almost as alive as a human being. This was particularly true of the Highlands, where no stretch of ground was dull.

The Gaelic scholar John MacInnes writes:

The native Gael, who is instructed in poetry, carries in his imagination not so much a landscape, not a sense of geography alone, nor of history alone, but a formal order of experiences in which all these are merged.

What is to a stranger an expanse of empty countryside – magnificent or drab according to prevailing notions – to the native sensibility can be dynamic, even heroic, territory peopled with figures from history and legend.

The great heritage of stories of witches and warriors, of human beings being transformed into horses or deer, of faeries and water horses, all helped people towards a deep love of landscape and an intimate knowledge of nature. It is argued that a legacy of this is still 'in the air', so to speak, and influences some people today.

To understand some modern claims to psychic experiences in the hills, it is helpful to examine the way of life of past times. It was pastoral and not urban. Life would often be hard, war was frequent (and martial virtues admired), but very early Gaelic poetry, song and story often shows an exquisite appreciation of the beauties of landscape. There were blemishes, such as wholesale hacking down of woodland, but in most cases – and certainly including the shieling pattern – life was environmentally friendly.

It is easy in a book such as this to stray into examining Highland life as a whole, or to investigate all of Celtic nature lore, but suffice it to say that hills, moors, glens, straths, woods and coastlines were loved by the people. They relished them with an impressive degree of cultural sophistication which gives the lie to critics from other cultures who call them uncivilised, backward or barbarian simply because of a difference in language.

Although their landscape was besprinkled with tales of ghosts and sprites and the people firmly believed that good or bad spirits lived in different trees or plants, their life had much joy in it. 'The soul of the Gael is on the summit of the mountain,' exults the Gaelic proverb.

Here were people whose year was mainly divided into four – Beltane, the Celtic spring, and the great November feast of Samhainn when cattle were separated for slaughter or breeding and the end of the grazing season. Two other feasts were Imbolc (February), which marked the beginning of lactation in ewes, and Lugnasad (August), the harvesting of crops.

At Beltane (see page 43), the Celtic spring, cleansing fires were lit on special hills.

When the new moon appeared men bowed and women curtsied – they were not worshipping the moon, but creation and the earth's cycles. Men and women went to the highest hill to see the moon, the *rioghainn na h-oidhche*, or Queen of the Night, and began their scrutiny in the west, turning slowly on the right heel until the moon was seen.

The same ritual was performed in honour of the sun and particularly so when it was linked to the Christian feast of Easter. Some people climbed to the top of their highest hill before sunrise and reflected on the God who made the smallest blade of grass grow – the same God who made the massive sun move.

These actions replaced pagan sun worship and are reflected in our own day with annual Easter services on prominent hills. Similarly, the practice of some mountaineers of going up suitable hills to see the sun rise, such as Ben Vorlich at south Loch Earn, in Perthshire, also has its roots here, although nowadays it is carried out around midsummer.

The sacred force in ancient stones and water was recognised and some hill slopes contained wells with medicinal powers. Christianity latterly and gradually influenced nature lore, as in the custom where hill people drank three mouthfuls of water from the confluence of three burns while invoking the Christian Trinity of Father, Son and Holy Ghost to ward off evil.

It is not too mystical or fanciful to say that some hillwalkers can sit and listen to the sounds and scents of the hills and feel a sense of oneness; a timeless intimacy. If they stopped to analyse it they would feel 'possessed'. The hills speak to them.

Nan Shepherd, in her book *The Living Mountain: A Celebration of the Cairngorm Mountains of Scotland* (1977) wrote:

> I believe that I now understand in some small measure why the Buddhist goes on Pilgrimage to a mountain. The journey is itself part of the technique by which the god is sought.
>
> It is a journey into Being; for, as I penetrate more deeply into the mountain's life, I penetrate also into my own.
>
> For an hour I am beyond desire. It is not ecstasy, that leaps out of the self that makes man like a god. *I am not out of myself, but in myself.* I am. To know Being, *this is the final grace accorded from the mountain.*

Much of this can sound so esoteric as to occasionally verge on the ridiculous, but there is truth in it. People have different wavelengths to 'supernatural' or near-psychic events; different levels of receptivity to 'the spirit of nature' – to the effect of hill scenery and landscape.

The old tales and legends of ghosties and goblins have gone the way of all folklore in many countries in our age of science, but the legends which I have included in this book – such as the story of Diarmaid and Grainne – still linger as faint echoes among the hills.

Such tales were once told at the shielings whose sites are well known to all hill-goers – little clusters of stones, often in delectable spots, the foundations of the temporary spring and summer homes of the people which were built from turf and heather.

It can be argued with conviction that experiences of supernatural beings or of telepathy or of 'mind links' with long-vanished races are rare in our own day. I think the reason for that lies in the nature of our hill world nowadays. When hills and glens were quiet, tranquil and peaceful, then the hill person could really find solitude, and senses were heightened and psychic phenomena and mind-links with the past could be more readily absorbed.

Additionally, from time to time, if the veil is to be turned back for modern people to access the thought processes of the ancient generations, then the atmosphere and the setting has got to be a fitting and an appropriate one and the person reasonably receptive, even although he or she may not consciously realise that.

The best-known spectre of all is Am Fear Liath Mór, The Big Grey Man of Ben MacDhui, in the Cairngorms, of whom nothing has been heard for many years. Yet at one time relatively modern mountaineers were wary of going to that hill.

Our mountains are busy places nowadays. Numbers going to the hills for 'recreation' (an inadequate word) continue to grow, although in Scotland, with a population of five million and much land where the hand of man is least evident, it would always eventually level out – even with increased tourism.

The Big Grey Man of Ben MacDhui will never return to that mountain. The mountain is too busy. It is often thronged with people. The old mystery has gone.

There is no longer an atmosphere when the feel of the hill can frighten people. There is too much modern static between people and the way past hillmen and women regarded their beliefs and feeling.

A modern door has opened and through it has passed, for millions of people and perhaps for ever, the ghosts of the past.

The modern hillwalkers who state they have 'seen' people appear and vanish or heard inexplicable noises, or who have had telepathic contact, are fortunate people indeed. They have experienced in our own day a dimension of the past for a few fleeting moments.

I believe such experiences will become more rare or will disappear as our hill world changes and becomes more noisy, more managed and developed. The astonished people who have been involved in inexplicable incidents should cherish them for they are special.

CHAPTER ONE

THE TRUTH IS GREY

The Big Grey Man of Ben MacDhui is the best-known spectre of the Scottish mountains and he is also the one of which the most nonsense is talked. He is a puzzle and yet he may hold the key to at least partly answering why so many alleged spectres have disappeared from Scottish hills in modern times.

It is often said that reports of the Grey Man, *Am Fear Liath Mór* in Gaelic, do not go back very far, but the truth is that the Cairngorms in the region of Glen More, Loch Morlich, Ben MacDhui, Loch Avon and the Lairig Ghru, have many legends telling of spectres of several kinds.

It is often said that Professor Norman Collie, who began the outburst of modern interest in the Grey Man, was so afraid when he saw the Grey Man that he ran away. But Collie did not *see* anything.

Once upon a time, Ben MacDhui, at 4,296 ft the highest mountain in the Cairngorms, was hard to get at, but with a modern road up Glen More and a ski and tourism chairlift to the plateau of Cairngorm, it is now easily reached by many people and its supernatural mystique has become eroded.

Dr Collie, first Professor of Organic Chemistry at the University of London, said in a speech in New Zealand that he had had an odd experience on Ben MacDhui in 1891. Interest in Britain in this anecdote did not increase until he repeated his speech in 1925 at the twenty-seventh annual general meeting in Aberdeen of the Cairngorm Club, Scotland's oldest mountaineering club, of which he was honorary president.

Aberdeenshire-born Dr Collie was a Fellow of the Royal Society and a mountaineering pioneer. He recalled:

I was returning from the cairn on the summit in a mist when I began to think I heard something other than merely the noise of my own footsteps.

For every few steps I took I heard a crunch, and then another crunch as if something was walking after me, but taking steps three or four times the length of my own. I said to myself, 'This is all nonsense'. I listened and heard it again, but could see nothing in the mist. As I walked on and the eerie crunch, crunch, sounded behind me, I was seized with terror and took to my heels, staggering blindly among the boulders for four or five miles nearly down to Rothiemurchus Forest. Whatever you make of it I do not know, but there is something very queer about the top of Ben MacDhui and I will not go back there again by myself I know.

It must be firmly lodged that Dr Collie had a mild reputation for being a prankster. Nevertheless, but for his speeches, there would probably be no modern interest in the Big Grey Man.

Others, however, came forward. Dr A.M. Kellas, who died on the 1921 Mount Everest reconnaissance expedition, heard of Dr Collie's experience and contacted him, describing how he had *seen* a 'big grey man' on Ben MacDhui. Dr Kellas left no written account, but a friend of his brother Henry, Mr W.G. Robertson, wrote to the *Press and Journal* newspaper in December 1925 saying that Dr Kellas and his brother had been chipping for crystals in the late afternoon well below the cairn when they saw a giant figure. They ran away and it allegedly pursued them into Corrie Etchachan. There was mist at the time.

Mr Robertson insisted that Dr Kellas's integrity was beyond question, but this account is not clear evidence. It is second-hand. Mr Robertson said that the incident could not be explained by critics saying that the sun had thrown the shadow of a figure on to the mist which magnified it. If that had happened, then *two* figures would have been seen.

Others have told of strange feelings when on Ben MacDhui – the feeling of being accompanied by another mysterious person. Many people who have indulged in solo hillwalking know the feeling of having an unseen companion or the sound of distant burns sounding like voices. Others have heard a single, high-pitched note or noises like music, but that, too, can be explained by atmospheric pressure, a cold in the head or illness.

There are other detailed accounts of the apparition, but most are anonymous and, therefore, lose much of their value. One such speaks of a huge brown creature swaggering down the mountain and by measuring its height using an ice axe and nearby boulders it was reckoned to be between 24 and 30 feet high.

Experienced mountaineer, photographer and writer Alexander Tewnion wrote in the *Scots Magazine* of June 1958 that in October 1943 he had gone climbing by himself in the Cairngorms and he had taken his wartime revolver with him in the hope of shooting game to eke out his rations. When he was descending the Corrie Etchachan track in a storm, he heard footsteps behind him and when a strange shape loomed up and charged at him he drew his revolver and fired three shots at it. He outpaced it down the hill and was quite convinced he had encountered the Big Grey Man.

It is widely known that 'footsteps' can be caused by warm air in contact with low temperatures. Condensation is created which is projected in water 'bombs' which land and make track marks, or the wind can make shrieking noises in the rocks. Boulders can look like monsters in the mist or in poor light. Snow creaks and cracks.

Nevertheless, mountaineer and writer Philip Tranter, son of historian and novelist Nigel Tranter, and who was killed in a car accident in France in 1966, summed it up for many people when he wrote: 'I myself am quite neutral on the subject . . . those who have seen Ferla Mor [note: this is incorrect Gaelic] include some who are neither ignorant, credulous, inexperienced nor uninformed.'

The much respected mountaineer, writer and conservationist, W.H. Murray, wrote: 'That Norman Collie had a psychic experience on Ben MacDhui is (for me) certain. To ascribe the cause to a Fear Liath Mór is, however, quite another matter.'

There has certainly been a great deal written on the subject and those interested in pursuing details of other experiences linked to the Ben MacDhui mystery should read Affleck Gray's magisterial book. In 1949 the Edinburgh Psychic College published a booklet which included 'experiences' on Ben MacDhui.

Sir Walter Scott mentions the *Boda Glas* (Bodach Glas) or Grey or Dark Man, in his novel of the 1745 Jacobite Rising, *Waverley*, and it appeared before Highland chiefs as a prediction of death. Others believe the spectre is an ancestor of the Mackenzies of Whitewell. Others again, heap scorn on the whole thing.

Seton Gordon, naturalist, historian, writer and Cairngorms expert, wrote that there *was* a Grey Man tradition. He was locally believed to be the ghost of Uilleam Ruighe Naoimhe, William Smith, the Cairngorms poet, whose song, 'Allt an Lochain Uaine' (The Burn of the Small Green Loch) was sung in the district into living memory.

Seton Gordon wrote:

One of the people of the district who saw the spectre told me that the day was cold and stormy, with snow squalls. As the narrator of the event was crossing the plateau to Coire an t-Sneachda, a man of greyish complexion was seen to be following, and although the day was bitterly cold, he was in his shirt sleeves with no coat on him. When the edge of the corrie was reached, the mysterious figure disappeared. There was nothing disquieting in this apparition except the strangeness of his dress on that snowy day, and his sudden uncanny disappearance.

Writer and Scottish patriot Wendy Wood writes in her book *The Secret of Spey* that when she was in the Lairig Ghru in 1940 – a time when she had no knowledge of either Dr Collie's or Dr Kellas's experiences – she heard an enormous echoing voice which seemed to use Gaelic words. It occurred to her that it might be the barking of a deer magnified by a freak echo. Latterly, the sound seemed to come from beneath her feet.

She began searching the snow in an ever-widening circle in case the sound came from an injured climber. Then she had an uneasy feeling of someone following her and taking gigantic strides. She ran away and did not pause until close to Whitewell when the barking of a dog brought her to her senses.

But what of the other spectres? Tom Crowley, president of Moray Mountaineering Club in the early 1920s, said that he was descending from Braeriach to Glen Einich when he saw a huge, grey figure with pointed ears, long legs and feet with talons. He heard footsteps and fled.

A red-handed spectre once haunted Glen More. Sir Walter Scott brought the spectre into his epic poem *Marmion* and he wrote that the glen was haunted by a spirit called *Làmh Dhearg* who was clad in the array of an ancient warrior who had a bloody hand from which he took his name. The spectre insisted on fighting all those he met. One of the tasks of *Làmh Dhearg* was to supply human sacrifice and protect the deer.

Another spectre, *Bodach a' Chleocain Dheirg*, the Carlin of the Little Red Cloak, lived near Coylum Bridge and was a 'goodie', helping travellers on their way. The River Nethy, which has its source high in the Cairngorms, was believed to be haunted by water sprites. The Shaws of Rothiemurchus sheltered a sprite named *Bodach an Dùin*, the Old Man of the Doune. When the Grants took possession of the property, *Bodach an Dùin* left the house and guarded the tomb of the Shaws in Rothiemurchus burial ground.

The Grants of Tullochgorm also had a spectral being – a boy called *Mag Molach*, meaning hairy. His left hand was covered in hair and he is sometimes erroneously referred to as Meg Mulloch. He lit a candle to show people the way home.

John Burton, a native of Deeside, writing in 1864, said that the people believed a giant patrolled the Lairig Ghru and waved a fir-tree in his hand as a kind of club. He could enlarge his head and shrink his body and was given the name of *Famh*, probably derived from the Gaelic *famhair*, meaning mole catcher or giant. The name *famh* is also Gaelic for mole. Indeed, it was widely held that as well as the club-wielding giant, a supernatural mole, the size of a large dog, haunted the glens of the Cairngorms.

James Hogg, the Ettrick Shepherd (1722–1835), whose literary star is happily rising again in our own day, visited Ben MacDhui during his second Highland journey. Hogg had a deep interest in the occult and he wrote of the *famh* gliding over the fell in his poem *Glen Avin* in *The Queen's Wake*.

The old *Statistical Account* says people believed that it left a slimy trail behind it, particularly in the early part of the day, which was later dispelled by sunlight. The grass in Glen Einich was believed to be poisonous for horses and this was attributed to the slime of the *famh*.

Other local tales speak of the 'paw calf', the *magh-ghamhainn* – a rough, dark, grisly monster which lived in the same area. This may have been a bear.

Hogg was also told that a spectre or ghost had been responsible for the famous tragedy at Gaick, above Dalnacardoch, in Badenoch, when, in the first week of January 1800, five men died when an avalanche buried their shelter. The *Scots Magazine* of 1800 recorded that: 'Captain [referred to in some accounts as Major] Macpherson of Lorick, and four other gentlemen, unfortunately perished in a storm of snow, when on a shooting party on the Duke of Gordon's grounds in Badenoch.'

The area was feared by local people as a haunt of demons. Captain John Macpherson, a recruiting officer, and his shooting party friends, were sheltering in a substantial lodge when the avalanche struck. Part of the walls were carried four hundred yards away and their guns were twisted out of shape. Three hunting dogs also died.

James Hogg was one of the first to put the tragedy into print in November 1810. He said Macpherson had been guilty of cruelty and injustice in rounding up deserters and in raising recruits and that the local people detested him.

Hogg wrote that Macpherson had visited Gaick earlier in the week and had been threatened by a mysterious stranger who had made a spectre-like exit. It was widely believed in the area that the tragedy was the work of a demon.

The roots of the Grey Man almost certainly lie in a folk tradition of monsters and spectres, and its image would have had no more modern public prominence than the red-handed and red-cloaked spectres of Glen More had it not been for Norman Collie.

A scientist, and widely respected as a mountaineer, he gave his key speeches at a time when mountains were only gradually being opened up for formal sport although their passes, summits and recesses had been known to the Gaelic people for centuries.

The outstanding expert, by far, on the Grey Man is 88-year-old Affleck Gray, of Pitlochry; a man who knows the Cairngorms intimately. Affleck produced the definitive book on the controversy, *The Big Grey Man of Ben MacDhui: Myth or Monster*, which wades through all the theories and psychic phenomena – the mist, wind, the Brocken Spectre, temperature changes, Gaelic lore, ley lines, hysteria, publicity hunters, the Abominable Snowman, extra-terrestrial beings, reincarnated spirits, a Buddhist presence in the Lairig Ghru and levitated Tibetan lamas meeting in a cave on Ben MacDhui.

'I think there *is* something peculiar about Ben MacDhui, but I don't think it is supernatural,' Affleck says. He knows and loves his hills and has only experienced one 'odd' happening himself when the door on the old Corrour bothy, once more sophisticated than the present spartan shelter, opened and shut on its own.

There was no wind and no one in the vicinity and he spent ages trying to get the door to do that again of its own volition. He had called out a greeting because he thought a person was coming through the door. He tried bumping the jambs of the door with his shoulder and creating vibration by jumping up and down, but to no avail. Other than that, he believes that most 'sightings' have a natural explanation or are in the mind.

CHAPTER TWO

THE DEFILE OF DREAD

If anyone claims seeing a ghost or spectre, the first question to be asked is generally about the character of the witness and the second is about the weather conditions of the time.

Himalayan and Alpine climber and writer Frank Smythe 'saw' a massacre in the Highlands in 1942 and wrote an account of it. Frank Smythe was one of the world's finest mountaineers and was experienced in the 'feel' of the Scottish hills. At the time, he was based at Braemar, near the Cairngorms, and held the rank of Squadron Leader as he had been appointed to command a Forces unit teaching mountain warfare to Commandos in the Cairngorms.

He went to Kintail, in the north-west of Scotland, on leave and decided to walk to the spectacular Falls of Glomach. The Falls are among the most impressive in Scotland although not – as it is sometimes said – the highest (that honour belongs to Eas an Coulin, near Kylesku, Sutherland). Glomach means dark, gloomy or forbidding.

He writes in his book, *The Mountain Vision*, that he entered a grassy, sun-warmed defile. He does not name a specific spot, but the most likely site is the Bealach na Sròine, the pass-of-the-nose. To the south of the Falls lies the Bealach an Sgàirne – a name which can translate as a pass where the rocks make noises, that is, the wind 'sighs' or screeches through them; or the stones make clattering noises.

He felt an aura of evil as if something terrible had once happened there, but he firmly decided to halt for lunch, to smoke a pipe and throw off the feeling. The eerie sense of foreboding persisted, however, and he suddenly saw a score or more of ragged people, men, women and children, straggling through a little ravine or cleft.

They appeared very weary, as though they had come a long way. The pitiful procession was in the midst of the defile when all of a sudden from either side concealed men leapt to their feet and, brandishing spears, axes and clubs, rushed down with wild yells on the unfortunates beneath. There was a short fierce struggle, then a horrible massacre. Not one man, woman or child was left alive: the defile was choked with corpses. I got out of the place as quickly as I could. Screams seemed to dim my ears as I hastened down the broad heather slopes into Glen Glomach.

I am not a superstitious person, but it seemed to me that I was vouchsafed a backward glimpse into a blood-stained page of Highland history. I know nothing about the history of that part of Scotland and should be grateful for any information throwing light on what I believe was a genuine psychical experience.

It is said in mountaineering circles that people have seen ghostly figures in Glen Shiel, believed to be those of Spaniards who fought on the Jacobite side in the Battle of Glen Shiel in the short-lived Rising of 1719, but I can find no 'first source'.

Frank Smythe had a follow-up correspondence with Affleck Gray, when Affleck was researching his own book, but Frank Smythe could not add to his account of the event.

It is tempting to speculate that a place where the Gaelic name makes clear that the wind makes noises in the stones might well account for Frank Smythe hearing screams, but it would not be sufficient to explain the incident away. (The lochan on Lochnagar, near Ballater, was originally called Loch na Gàire, Loch of the Outcry, because the wind moaned among the rocks.) However, Frank Smythe was accustomed to all the noises and sounds of the hill world and he did not have misty conditions.

He later wrote to *The Scotsman* saying that he had been told a massacre had taken place between Morvich and Glen Glomach either in the 1715 and 1745 Jacobite Risings or afterwards, but he did not think there was any link. The site and details of dress and weapons did not fit.

There *have* been some odd happenings in the area. Elizabeth Sutherland writes in the National Trust for Scotland booklet, *Balmacara, Kintail and the Falls of Glomach* (published in 1952), that two climbers coming down into Gleann Choinneachain (the mossy glen) claimed a memorable 'sighting'.

They passed a tall, thin, white-bearded man with a cape over his kilt, holding the hand of a small girl dressed in a cloak and hood. They made local inquiries and found the description fitted the ghosts of Osgood Hanbury Mackenzie, creator of the famed Inverewe gardens (who died in 1922) and his daughter, Mhairi. They were both great walkers and loved Kintail.

Brenda Macrow, mountaineer, poet and writer, points out in her book *Kintail Scrapbook*, written just after the Second World War, that the Glomach area is rich in tales of faeries – a ghostly washerwoman, a 'blue lady' seen by shepherds, and other apparitions.

It was widely believed in past centuries that some Kintail people had strange powers.

CHAPTER THREE

PUZZLE BY THE BURN

An extraordinary occurrence took place on the Gaick (pronounced gike) estate in the 1950s, that long glen and isolated lodge lying amid steep-sided hills to the east of the modern A9 and south of Blair Atholl.

The old Gaick lodge became notorious when an avalanche killed five men in 1800. The area is rich in tales of faery people and also of a giant fish, the Dorman, which was believed to inhabit Loch an t-Seilich not far from the lodge and which allegedly prevented salmon from the River Tromie reaching the loch.

It is against that background of black tragedy and legend that Colonel Jimmy Dennis went stalking one autumn and shot a stag in the area behind the new lodge. Because the afternoon was fine, he asked the ponyman to take the stag down and he lingered on, enjoying the views.

As he sat there, he became aware of a movement at the head of the burn which ran below him in the glen. At first he thought it was a roe-deer because it had a rusty or chestnut-red look. It was moving quietly about the green moss and flat stones that surrounded the spring.

When he scoured the spot with his telescope (preferred by many stalkers to binoculars) he could see nothing.

Puzzled, he examined the ground again.

He found he could see the moving object with his naked eye, but not with the telescope. By shading his brow, he could make out that the creature was of human form and he later described it as like a child in a siren suit and pixie hood. He decided to try and get closer, but the moment he moved forward, the object vanished and never reappeared. Colonel Dennis returned to the lodge mystified and, because of fear of ridicule, only told his wife.

In later years, when stalking in the neighbouring forest of Glen Bruar, he mentioned this odd experience to the stalker there who said, 'Then ye've seen the sprite of Gaick.'

An old legend of the area tells of a celebrated stalker called Murdoch who, in the 1800s, was out after hinds one morning when he saw several tiny women dressed in green, milking the deer.

One of the women had a hank of green wool thrown over her shoulder and, as she was milking the hind, it made a grab at the hank and swallowed it. The angered faery shouted that a dart from Murdoch's quiver would pierce the hind before nightfall.

Murdoch left the scene, but later – the tales say – when he shot a hind, it had the green wool in its stomach.

The only likely explanation to Colonel Dennis's friends was that he had some kind of psychic experience. He was too experienced a hillman in the ways of deer or weather to mistake the wind in the grasses, or tricks of the light, for a moving and apparently animate object. In any case, why did his telescope not focus on the object when it worked perfectly well on everything else?

CHAPTER FOUR

THE FIGHTING FIANNA

The great heroes and heroines of Celtic and Norse mythology lived as real people in the minds, souls and hearts of the communities who lived in the glens and straths in olden times. They were prominent in song and story and are commemorated in many hill names.

At Kilmuir, in Skye, a trap dyke or wall runs up a steep incline and local people called it the Wall of the Fianna (Garadh na Feinne) and some Skye hills have viewpoints called the Chair or Seat of Fionn. On Beinn Iadain, in Morvern, there are steps in the rocks near the summit known as Ceumannan Fhinn or Fingal's Steps. Beinn na Greine, Mountain of the Sun, above Portree, in Skye, was reputed to be a place where Fionn sunbathed while watching his warriors below.

The key ones are Fionn, or Fingal, the great warrior god, his son, Ossian or Oisin (pronounced oh-shin) and his grandson, Oscar, and the band of warriors and hunters known as the Fianna or Fingalians. (Their name is also given as the Feinne.)

The Gaelic word *fionn* means white or fair. Fionn Mac Cumhail, known in English as Fingal or Finn MacCoul, was the leader of the Fianna and also appears in Norse legend. His name is also given as Feinn which can mean giant, warrior or hero.

There are two strands to such beliefs – one of the imagination and one of reality.

Fionn was very probably based on a real person, a warrior of ancient Gaeldom in Scotland and Ireland, skilled in arms and learning, who became the giant of legend who flung part of Ireland into the sea to become the Isle of Man. He is also reputed to have built the Giant's Causeway from Northern Ireland to Scotland to fight a Scottish giant.

The old tales of these heroes may have been the root of later Arthurian legend and the Fianna may be the forerunners of the knights of the Round Table.

Fionn Mac Cumhail was believed to have leaped over the Cuillin of Rum and landed in the western sea – which was known as a place where Fionn washed his feet.

Fingalian giants also had a habit of tossing boulders around which local people noted and regarded with affection. These included hills like Bennachie, in the north-east, and the so-called Samson's Stone on the lower slopes of Ben Ledi, near Callander, in Perthshire.

Fionn also had favourite hunting dogs, Bran and Luath, long popular as names of stalkers' and shepherds' dogs, and they too are commemorated in hill names. Some prominent standing stones were tethering posts for their hounds.

The Fingalians or Fianna were great hunters and could cover huge distances in the chase. They only ate one meal a day for which they gathered on a chosen hill. Afterwards, they bathed in home-made saunas of stone, turf and huge fires.

The famous glacial scores on the hillsides of Glen Roy, in Lochaber – the so-called Parallel Roads which are nowadays classified as a site of special scientific interest and in the care of Scottish Natural Heritage – were thought to be the hunting roads of the Fianna which had echoed to the rumble of their chariots.

According to legend, a cave in Glen Orchy in Argyll has an ancient hunting horn on the wall. Whoever finds it should blow it and out of the graves, travelling over the centuries, the Fingalian warriors will rise and come to aid Scotland in the hour of her need.

There are tales of the Fianna in Glen Coe and Glen Etive. King Earragan, of Lochlann, the old name for Scandinavia, warred against them. He sailed up Loch Leven and camped in the area called Laroch, near Invercoe House. The Fianna camped in a wood on the lower slopes of Sgurr nam Fiannaidh. They dug ditches and were screened by trees. Stones from Sgor na Ciche, the Pap of Glen Coe, were hurled at the invaders.

A Christian aspect to such folklore tells of the Celtic saint, Kenneth, who lived in a sunless part of Glen Coe. An angel offered to remove the mountain and cast it into the sea, but St Kenneth refused to allow this.

However, the Aonach Eagach ridge, the best ridgewalk in Scotland outwith Skye, which bounds the north side of the glen, has a fissure in the rocks which was created when the angel started his task.

Glen Geusachan, in the eastern Cairngorms, was the traditional hunting-ground of the Fianna and a deep corrie above the glen is called Coire Cath nam Fiann – Corrie of the Battle of the Fingalians. Beinn Bhrotain is not far away and is reputed to take its name from a jet-black hound which chased the white faery deer and which was owned by the Fianna.

On Ben Avon an old legend persisted that Fingal's wife, The Very Fair One, went to Clach Bhàn to bathe in one of its rock pools. Pregnant women who were near confinement used to visit Clach Bhàn and sit in one of the worn potholes in the belief that it would ensure easy labour, and this custom lingered on late into the last century.

The ford on the A'an below Loch A'an (Avon) is called Ath nam Fiann – the Ford of the Fingalians – and is part of the second-best known Cairngorms pass, the Lairig an Laoigh.

The names and association-sites are like memorials in the hills . . . on Mull there is Torr nam Fiann, the conical hill of the Fingalians . . . the warrior queen Sgathach of Skye is commemorated in Dùn Sgàthaich (Dunscaith), a hill fort near Tokavaig, at the mouth of Loch Eishort, in Sleat, a name which may mean 'the shadowy one'. She was held in such high esteem that warriors, including the famous Cuchulain, knight of the Red Branch of Ulster, travelled from Ireland for tuition in the arts of war. Another warrior queen who ruled the hills of Morvern is also remembered.

Horseshoe-shaped holes or marks on the Slabs, the great boiler plates of rock on Ben Trilleachan, above Loch Etive, in Argyll, which provide rock-climbs of great exposure and severity, were believed to have been made by Cuchulain's horse when it leaped from Ben Starav on the other side of the glen.

Tradition has it that the island of Arran was the home of Manannan Mac Lir, the God of the Sea, and it enjoyed a reputation as a land of paradise, like Tir nan Og – the land beyond the sea where all was golden and youth was everlasting.

The hunters of the Fianna came to Arran to hunt deer.

Arran of the many stags,
The sea strikes against its shoulder,
Isle where companies are fed,
Ridge on which blue spears are reddened

One of the peaks which rises from Glen Sannox, Suidhe Fhearghais – the Seat of Fergus – is named after the poet of the Fianna, known as Fergus of the True Lips.

CHAPTER FIVE

OSSIAN AND OSCAR

Our hill lochs have many tales of water horses – the king of the beasts in Gaelic folklore – and some stories of children being drowned by riding on water horses probably have a basis in real accidents.

It was widely believed that beneath the seas and inland lochs lay the dwellings of people and another living world. To girls out gathering cattle on the hill, the *each-uisge*, the water horse, would sometimes appear as a young man and they had to be wary if they saw sand in his hair.

Ossian, the bard-son of Fingal, was taken to the Land of the Young by the Golden Haired Niamh, a goddess from the otherworld, and they rode on a stallion and a white horse under the water.

Ossian or, more properly, Oisian or Oisin, is a diminutive of *os*, meaning deer. He was a great warrior and married Eibhir, who was one of the most beautiful women in the world, and he is commemorated in many hill sites. The most prominent of these is Ossian's Cave, on Aonach Dubh, in Glen Coe – a great slash in the rocky face of the mountain. It has a sloping floor and at one time contained a tin box into which climbers put their names. Ossian is reputed to be buried in the Sma' Glen, south of Amulree, Perthshire.

The writings of James Macpherson (1738–96), who was born in Kingussie and is buried in Westminster Abbey, caused a literary sensation in the eighteenth century when he claimed to have found an unknown store of classic and heroic Gaelic literature – a controversy which is still with us. Some of the poems were ancient fragments, some his own composition and some a mixture of both. He became known as 'Ossian Macpherson' and the poems led to 'heroic' follies in the style of the writings being erected by the Duke of Atholl at The Hermitage, near Dunkeld: a site now in the care of the National Trust for Scotland.

Oscar, the son of Ossian and grandson of Fingal, is not as prominent among our hill names as the rest of the family, but he does appear. He was the mightiest warrior of the Fianna and commanded a battalion called 'The Terrible Broom' because it swept its enemies from the field. His name is derived from the Norse Asgeirr, occasionally spelled Osgar, and means divine spear.

The rock called Clach Oscar, near the mouth of Abhainn an t-Stratha Mhóir at the head of Loch Slapin, and in the Torrin area of Skye, is not large, and is now split, but it had a special importance for island people long ago. It was a ringing rock, sending out bell-like notes when correctly struck, and is one of a number of similar ringing rocks in Scotland. Oscar is believed to have hurled it there from Beinn Dearg Mhór in order to kill a monster in Loch na Sguabaidh.

CHAPTER SIX

SNAKES AND SERPENTS

It was small, black, angry looking and uncharacteristically truculent. Adders tend to be retiring beasts, only wanting to be left alone, although they are sometimes slow at sliding away and avoiding the boots of passing hillwalkers. This one, though, for reasons best known to itself, lay in the middle of the forest track north of Conic hill on the West Highland Way and close to Loch Lomond.

We gave it a very gentle prod with a stick to try and help it wriggle to the side of the path, but it continued to rear up and face us. Eventually with the help of a large piece of bark and a long piece of wood, we transferred it to the undergrowth at the side of the track. I was going up The Merrick, in Galloway, with my son, Tom, and was slightly ahead of him on the path when he called me back. I had walked past an adder without noticing it, but the thud of my boots had made it move and Tom saw it.

Adders, our only poisonous snake, have an undeserved reputation for being harmful, yet more people have died from bee stings or dog attacks over the years than from the bite of an adder. In Britain, there have probably been no more than twelve fatalities from adder bites in a century. There are many highly experienced hillwalkers who have never seen an adder and it is often a lottery if one does so. Apart from this experience, I have only encountered the reptile three times in 40 years of exploring Scotland's hills.

Captain Ronnie Leask, of Edinburgh, a master mariner, historian and hill tramper, found a dead one when we spent a long weekend at the north end of Jura. And Fred Gordon, a senior Ranger with Gordon district council and a mountaineer of great experience, 'bumped' one when he and I were in Glen Gairn, the back way in from the Ballater road to these fine mountains, Beinn a' Bhùird and Ben Avon. It, too, lay obligingly on the path and we photographed it at our ease and compared it to the size of our boots. The third occasion was when my son, Tom, and I saw an adder near the Queen's Well, at the foot of Mount Kean.

Sometimes people claim they have seen an adder when, in fact, they have seen the harmless grass snake or the legless lizard, the slowworm. All British snakes are now protected in law, but such was the adder's unfair reputation that when it was given legal protection in 1991 some people wrote letters of protest to newspapers.

The fear of the snake is very old and some Celtic tales of sea beasts or huge serpents which inhabited parts of the Highlands may have their root in this fear.

It shows up in some place names, such as Coire na Béiste, hollow of the beast, as on Mull, or in hill names such as Meall na Nathrach Móire, the Hill of the Big Snake (Adder) on the fringe of Rannoch Moor. There are several hills around which reflect the name Nathrach, meaning 'of the adder'.

Generally, if you spy a snake in Scotland, it will usually be an adder. The legless lizard or slowworm is about the same length, around two feet, but tends to be smooth and shiny while the adder's skin is rough. Snakes cannot close their eyes so if the snake winks, it is a slowworm.

The adder can strike with rapidity and some people have been the target of an adder attack on their boots or socks and have never known it. The paired fangs are hollow and poison from two venom glands is pushed along them into the victim's body.

The twisting line of the serpent is strong in Celtic and Pictish design, perhaps demonstrating the intricacies and interdependence of living things. There may also be links with the Biblical story of the serpent bringing evil to paradise as Christian elements gradually became intermingled with the older forms and patterns of Celtic nature lore.

Tales of dragon-type beasts scoring mountain slopes and summits were not uncommon, and Beinn Vair (Beinn a' Bheithir) at Ballachulish, to the west of Glen Coe, though often translated as 'hill of the thunderbolt', can also mean a venomous blow – possibly from a serpent.

Glen More, on Mull, was reputed to be the place where an enormous serpent or snake once had its lair, and the largest adders were thought to live on Mull. Goats kept the numbers down, however, and then the arrival of the sheep in the nineteenth century did the same.

In the old calendar, St Bride's Day (*Feill Brìde*) fell on the first day of February (13 February by our modern calendar). St Bride was a mixture of Celtic saint and pagan goddess. The people of old believed that on that day, the serpent, the daughter of Ivor, emerged for the first time from her hole in the heather among the rocks. At the same time, the dandelion, 'the little notched flower of Bride', opened its first golden flower.

St Bride was believed to return to earth, coaxing life from the soil in the shape of spring flowers, as the goddess Brigit (Bride) had done before her.

Ivor may come from the name of a shadowy wife of an early constable of Eilean Donan castle, in Kintail, who dabbled in the occult, or from a wizard or a mysterious Celtic giant. A version of the old incantation says:

The Feast day of the Bride,
The daughter of Ivor shall come from the knoll,
I will not touch the daughter of Ivor,
Nor shall she harm me.

It was believed that the serpent or snake would not sting a descendant of Ivor, he having made *tabhar agus tuis* (offering and incense) to it, thereby securing immunity from its sting for himself and his seed for ever.

A propitiatory hymn was sung to the serpent and there are grounds for thinking it was venerated before it became an accursed thing after the coming of Christianity. In some variations of the hymn the snake was called the queen and may have symbolised the joining of male and female to create new life. Later, when it became a symbol of lust, greed or cunning, a piece of peat was put in a stocking and pounded with a stick to enact the crushing of the snake's head.

Alexander Carmichael tells in *Carmina Gadelica*, his magnificent nineteenth-century collection of Gaelic lore, of serpents' stones being found among the heather – especially in old, tall, unburned heather (which is rather harder to find today). The people believed the serpent or snake went round and round the clump of heather, emitting a froth or spittle from its mouth upon the clump and without pausing. When the spittle cooled and dried, the stuff grew as hard as a stone, but was very light, he said. It was about the size of a pullet's egg and dark grey.

Old people, he said, esteemed this 'egg' for its power in healing and its strength against faery women. It was good for curing swellings, cuts, or bruises or festering in a person. These adder stones or eggs were also supposed to provide magical protection.

Some so-called adder 'beads' are to be found in museums. It is now known that the hollow 'adder-stanes' are prehistoric spindle-wheels and highly coloured beads are of Iron Age glass.

That splendid Gaelic and folklore scholar, Mary Beith, whose articles are a joy in *The West Highland Free Press*, has speculated that it is just possible that snakes emerging from the holes where they have wintered might sometimes have dislodged long-buried ancient artifacts, thus giving rise to the legends.

In the Highlands it was held that second sight could be gained by taking the first taste of adder broo – a broth prepared from the body of a white snake. Snakes were used in potions by the great medical family of the Beatons, on Mull, and also by the noted Borders wizard, Michael Scott, and some sacred wells in the Highlands were reputed to be guarded by adders.

The Institute of Terrestrial Ecology at Banchory, in Grampian, conducted a survey of Scottish adders in 1993 and the ultimate verdict was that adder numbers were reasonably satisfactory.

St Bride and the daughter of Ivor will surely be content with that.

CHAPTER SEVEN

DANCING AND DEATH

Some hills leave the climber in an ecstasy of pleasure. They needn't be big – some of the best viewpoints in Scotland can be found on the small island hills.

The swelling and gentle mound of the Barr Mór on Lismore, sited like a green jewel at the mouth of Loch Linnhe, commands glorious views. It is only 127m. The same is true of the famous Sgurr of Eigg (393m), once the haunt of witches. It gave rise to the old Highland saying, 'I've been on the Sgurr of Eigg', meaning that the person speaking had a wide perspective of the issue under discussion.

The little hill on Muck, Beinn Airein (137m) is another, and so is the flat-topped Dùn Caan (443m) on the long island of Raasay, to the east of Skye.

James Boswell (1740–95), Samuel Johnson's biographer, colleague-traveller and near sycophant, visited Raasay from 8 to 12 September 1773 and climbed Dùn Caan. He was so taken by the breathtaking view of the Skye mountains, of sea and coastline, of the big mainland peaks of Applecross and Torridon, that he danced a jig of joy on Dùn Caan's smooth and flat top.

As all regular Skye-goers know, Dùn Caan's sawn-off peak is very prominent and, like Bennachie (pronounced bain-a-hee), in the north-east of Scotland, it is a marker for sailors. The word dun means, of course, a fort, but the meaning of the rest of the name produces arguments ranging from can-shaped to bonnet- or cap-shaped.

Boswell was a lawyer and an Anglicised Scot who entered London society. He became Dr Johnson's satellite and their tour of the Highlands and Islands in 1773 provides useful social commentaries on the times – although they made some howlers about Gaelic culture.

They found the stone-heads of prehistoric arrows on Raasay and were accurately told that the local people called them faery-bolts.

Boswell writes of passing two lakes close to Dùn Caan, one of which is called Loch na Mna – the loch of the woman. He was told that local people believed that a wild beast, a seahorse, had lived in it and that this beast had devoured a man's daughter. The man had then lit a large fire and had a sow roasted at it, the smell of which attracted the monster. The fire was placed on the side of the hill a little way down a hollow between Dùn Caan and another hill. A spit was put in the fire.

The man hid behind a little shelter of dry stones and made a kind of avenue for the monster with two rows of flat stones which led from the fire over the summit of the hill until it came to the side next to the loch. The monster wriggled or walked through the avenue and the man then destroyed it with the red hot spit.

Boswell was shown the hiding place and the stones. He was impressed by the serious way the tale had been presented to him.

There is a great puzzle here. A similar tale of roasting meat as bait for monsters is also told in other parts of the Highlands, but I wonder if there is not another explanation?

Could there have been confusion when translating a story from Gaelic into English? Did it accidentally grow in the telling? There is no physical evidence – no bones, etc. – to support it. Such was the regard and foreboding the people had for snakes or serpents is it just possible that the serpent was our humble adder and that the girl died from snakebite poison?

Because of the snake's exalted position, was it *ritually* killed with due ceremony rather than just being stamped on. Were the avenue of stones, the sacrificial meat (rather than bait), the cleansing power of fire, all used because a momentous act of destruction of a taboo, or a near-magical beast, took place? And later, did this near-sacred act become out of focus and grow in the telling over the years to be further misunderstood by Boswell?

CHAPTER EIGHT

THE MOUNTAINS OF GOD

Some experiences are unforgettable. We stood on the summit of Ben Vorlich, near Loch Earn, in Perthshire, and watched the eastern sky grow slowly lighter beyond far-off purple and black hills.

Then a blood-red line appeared for a few seconds above the horizon, followed by a quick apple-green band and then the sun came up in long, golden rays, lighting up the hillsides.

It was a magnificent sight and we were truly moved by the beauty of it. Tiny patches of morning mist began to peel up from the hillsides and we felt the warmth of the sun and all seemed alive, elemental, vital, golden and joyful.

It is not always easy to time and plan an expedition to see the sun coming up. Some hills, like Ben Cleuch in the Ochils, are popular for seeing the dawn breaking, but there are too many other hills in the way to have a far-off horizon and see the sun rise.

It is a good thing for hill people to do, not only because it can be entrancingly beautiful but because of its links with the past. It gives the sense of Beltane, the old Celtic new year, one of two main feasts in a four-seasons year. The other main one, Samhainn, in November, was when cattle were separated for slaughter or shelter and tail-end-of-the-year arrangements were made. It marked the end of the grazing season.

Beltane was held in May and signified the start of the warm days, of expectation of sunshine, the firm arrival of spring and the benevolent days of summer.

Even although most modern hill people have switched watching the sun rise from spring to summer, the roots of this idea lie in Beltane. They are very long roots and of all the hills in Scotland used as sites for pre- and post-Christian Beltane ceremonies, Ben Ledi, near Callander, in the

Southern Highlands, lays claim to being the most prominent site.

Ben Ledi stands out prominently from the blue wall of the Grampians when viewed from Stirling and the lower ground to the south. It has a special character and nowadays must be one of the most frequently ascended hills in Scotland, yet in the past it had a sacred significance.

The name Ledi *may* derive from *Beinn an Leothaid*, the mountain of the gentle slope – a reference to the long shoulder which runs down to Loch Venachar-side. But an alternative and more likely suggestion is *Beinn le Dia*, the mountain of God or Light.

It has an almost island-like setting, jutting forward from the main mass of the hills and bordered by two lochs. In view of its conspicuous situation, it's not surprising that Ben Ledi was picked out long ago as a special gathering ground when hundreds of young people from the glens, lochsides and townships round about headed for it at the beginning of May.

The Beltane Festival, *Latha Buidhe Bealltainn*, The Yellow Day of the Fires of Bel, probably has Druidic origins. However, people in Christian times from the parishes of Callander, Buchannan, Balquhidder and Aberfoyle still met on the summit to commemorate the lighting of the Bealltainn fires.

Bel derives from Be'uill, Life of All, an early Celtic sun god; and the colour yellow signifies gold and sunshine and good fortune. Funeral galleys on the Trossachs lochs used to describe a *deiseil* – a circle rowed three times sunwise – and this symbol of eternity, blessing and dedication is the form of the Celtic sun god. It is an idea handed down over thousands of years.

People long ago lived by a cattle economy and their seasonal pattern, their calendar, was dictated by this. Their ceremonies involved traditional food such as porridge and bannocks. In May the livestock went to the shielings pasturage on the higher ground and at the end of autumn returned to the byres or herbage near human settlement in the glens, straths and lochsides.

Customs linked to Beltane lingered on in Scotland well into the nineteenth century and some still exist in modern form, such as girls washing their faces in the May dew at dawn. Crowds still go up Arthur's Seat and the Calton Hill, in Edinburgh, to hail the sunrise and the modern growth of Easter services on hill summits has clear indications that the Christian belief in the Easter Resurrection replaced a Druidical pattern.

The origin of Beltane cannot be traced to ecclesiastical sources and predates Christianity.

It is easy to imagine chattering boys and girls walking in early May to the foot of Ben Ledi in late evening and then eventually huddling down on the summit in little groups, plaids tightly wrapped, while they waited for the dawn.

Back in their homes, cheese and butter were made before sunrise to ensure the faeries were kept away and no fire was given out to others for fear the borrower might be given power to spirit away milk from the lender's cows.

All hearth fires had already been extinguished and the Fire of Need, the *Teine Eigin*, was lit at dawn at Beltane and all the new house fires were rekindled from it. Bonfires were often kindled on the summits of hills.

There was a strong belief that witches, warlocks, faeries and other spirits held great gatherings at this time and had to be spiritually controlled. Rowan twigs, and branches from other 'good' trees, such as elder, juniper, or ash were made into crosses, tied with red thread, and put over doors.

The fires were lit as the sun rose and without the use of metal. An oak log was turned at speed in a hole in another log until sparks came and sometimes a kind of agaric which grows on old birches was then kindled and used to take the flame to other houses.

Cattle, sheep, goats and horses were driven between huge bonfires so that the smoke might remove evil spirits who might otherwise have brought disease or harm. In some places the herds were driven between fires, in others through the actual centres and people also jumped through, including parents carrying babies.

Sometimes torches were made of dried sedge or heather and were lit from the Beltane fire and carried to the people's own land and then carried round the boundary sunwise before being used to rekindle the hearth fire. In other areas, grassy mounds on moorland were chosen for sacred ceremonies.

On the grassy summit of Ben Ledi, the young people prepared bannocks from oatmal kneaded into a mixture of eggs and milk, and they were cooked on stones set in the ashes of fires. Sometimes a kind of custard was used. These were cut into portions and one piece was marked with charcoal. They were put into a bonnet and handed round. Whoever got the marked portion had to skip three times through the embers. People sometimes blackened their faces from the ashes.

This ceremony is believed to derive from far more elaborate rituals going back thousands of years and perhaps to human sacrifice. Its form varied greatly from district to district and the herdsmen sometimes symbolically offered pieces of bannock or cake to the fox, eagle, hoodie crow, wolf, raven and others in the hope that their calves or young goats, foals or lambs would be safe.

The late and lamented Dr Isobel F. Grant, historian, writer and founder of the Kingussie folk museum, Am Fasgadh, points out that these ceremonies were linked to fire worship and an ailing child was sometimes passed through a hoop of iron to which wisps of blazing straw were attached.

Caution was also needed. The third day of May was considered unlucky and was called *Latha Seachnaidh na Bliadhna*, the Avoiding Day of the Year. Celtic lore became intertwined with Christianity and it was considered bad luck to start important work or commit a sin because it was on the third day of summer that fallen angels were expelled from heaven.

The upper Stank Glen of Ben Ledi (the name derives from a Gaelic word for pools) contains huge boulders and pinnacle rocks on the steep hillside and local mountaineers sometimes sleep in nooks in the rocks. As night falls one can almost sense that in past times people rested or sheltered there before heading for the summit and the coming of the sun and to rejoice that Beltane, with all its promise, had arrived again.

CHAPTER NINE

LISTEN TO THE LADY

A time will come when Ben Lawers will become so cold that it will chill and waste the land around it for seven miles. So says one of the prophecies of the Lady of Lawers, *Baintighearna Labhair*, a Highland seer of the latter part of the seventeenth century. All but three of her prophecies have come to pass, the most recent in 1948. What might happen to Ben Lawers, one of the best-known mountains in Scotland, once the highest peak in Perthshire and now sited in Tayside region, is a mystery.

The Lady of Lawers's predictions have come down in oral tradition, but were also recorded in the *Red Book of Balloch* which was kept in the charter room of Taymouth Castle (at the east end of Loch Tay), but which is now missing. The castle mansion incorporates the ruins of an earlier castle, Balloch, once part of the lands of the expansionist Glen Orchy Campbells. The Lady is believed to have come from Appin as a bride to the small estate of Lawers about 1650. She was escorted by kinsfolk known as *Na Combaich*, the Companions.

The Lady of Lawers married the son of Sir James Campbell, sixth laird of Lawers, and they had a house on the shores of Loch Tay. Lawers was then an important site for the ferry to and from Ardtalnaig on the south shore of Loch Tay where a main route came over the hill from the Sma' Glen and Crieff. The remains of houses can still be seen.

A new church was built alongside the House of Lawers in 1669 and the Lady prophesied that 'the ridging stones will never be placed on the roof. If they are, then all my words are false.' A storm swept the carved, sandstone capping stones into deep water after they had been landed by barge and all were lost.

Her next prediction involved an ash tree which she planted on the north side of the church and alongside which one of her faithful Stewart servants, *An Combach Ruadh*, the Red-haired Companion, was buried. She said: 'The tree will grow and when it reaches the gable the church will be split asunder, and this will also happen when the red cairn on Ben Lawers falls.' The tree reached the gable in 1833 and a violent storm demolished the west loft of the church which fell into the middle of the building. It was then abandoned as a place of worship.

A cairn of red stones had been built on Ben Lawers by prospecting miners many years before and this collapsed in 1843 – the year of the famous Disruption in Scotland when the congregation of the area left the Church of Scotland and joined the Free Church over the issue of patronage and the independence of the clergy.

The Lady of Lawers's predictions were widely respected and heeded. She foretold: 'There will be a mill on every stream and a plough in every field and the two sides of Loch Tay will become a kail garden.' Kail, of course, means vegetables.

She said this in the years following the Marquis of Montrose's whirlwind campaign in the Scottish Wars of the Covenant in 1645 when the Royal army pillaged both sides of the loch. It took almost a century for the district to recover, but in the eighteenth century flax and new agricultural practices were introduced, many mills were built and the people flourished once more.

She also said that later the land would first be sifted and then riddled of its people. In 1834 the Marquis of Breadalbane evicted 55 families from the west end of Loch Tay and by 1838 another 60 families had been 'cleared' from Glen Quaich, near Amulree. These evictions were ruthless and were carried out to make way for sheep and the creation of sporting estates. Over 500 families were evicted and the lochside population fell from over 3,500 to around 100.

She predicted the demise of the House of Breadalbane and pinpointed the fate of leading individuals within it.

A carved stone once stood near the summit of Ben Lawers, which was stolen by an unknown person last century. It read: 'Spend as you get, and get as you spend. Save, and for whom? Remember death!' These words were also attributed to the Lady of Lawers.

Only three of her prophecies remain unfulfilled. A strange heir has still to come to Balloch (now Taymouth Castle) when the Boar's Stone at

Fearnan (a township on the north side of Loch Tay) topples over. The second causes some worry to the modern tourist board. 'A ship driven by smoke will sink in Loch Tay with great loss of life.' Lastly, her prediction about Ben Lawers chilling the ground round about is still discussed by mountaineers.

CHAPTER TEN

THE RUNAWAY LOVERS

The wild boar has long vanished from Scotland, but traces of it can still be seen on the carved stones of early peoples because its courage was greatly admired. It also features in hill and glen names which include the Gaelic word *tuirc* or *turc*, such as Carn an Tuirc, in Glen Shee, Perthshire, or villages like Brig o' Turk in the Trossachs where kings once hunted.

The boar also had legendary or mythical status and hillwalkers on Ben Gulabin (pronounced gool-abin), above Glen Shee and linking Glen Beag, who see a prominent gully running up the north side of the hill are often unaware that a famous wild boar once found refuge there. It is known in local tradition as 'the Boar's Bed'.

The heather slopes also have large 'scrapings' on them where little burns appear and vanish in rainstorms and these are reputed in legend to have been made by the boar's hooves.

Of all the ancient tales told in the winter townships or at the summer shielings one of the most popular was that of Diarmaid (pronounced deer-mutch) and Grainne (pronounced gran-yeh).

It comes in different versions and is told in both Scotland and Ireland and echoes of the story still reverberate in the hills on both sides of the sea. Our predecessors as hillmen and women did not treat such stories as 'tales'. They believed them to be true.

The banks of our rivers and large burns are often still shrouded with alder trees, long ago considered a dark tree of refuge and secrecy, and the tales portray Diarmaid and Grainne hiding in alder groves.

In the Scottish version of the old story, youthful Grainne was engaged (some accounts say married) to the elderly Fingal (Fionn or Fionn MacCumhail), the Celtic King-God. Oddly, her name may derive from the Irish word *grain*, hate or hatred.

She took a fancy to his nephew, Diarmaid, who was descended from the great house and race of O'Duibhne (Doon), after she saw him break up a fight between infuriated hounds, and was impressed by his courage. Diarmaid had a love spot (probably a birthmark) on his forehead or neck and this made him irresistible. He was known as Diarmaid of the Women.

Grainne bewitched him and put a sacred task, a *geas*, upon him, and persuaded him to elope with her, declaring she would die if he were to refuse. (Some accounts say she was originally in love with Ossian, the bard-son of Fingal, but was turned down.)

Fingal and his warriors pursued them and they left unbroken bread and uncooked salmon along the way, symbols that they had not yet slept together.

Aonghus Og, the love god and Diarmaid's foster father, aided them and hid Grainne under a cloak of concealment while the athletic Diarmaid leaped over the warriors of the Fianna and got away.

When they returned to the Royal court, the king, understandably, plotted Diarmaid's death. He invited Diarmaid to slay a wild boar of great ferocity which, in the Scottish version of the tale, had a lair on Ben Gulabin. (In the Irish version, this is Ben Bulben, in Co. Sligo.)

Diarmaid killed the boar, but it shredded his spear. He was ordered by the king to measure the boar with his bare foot from snout to tail and then to take the measurements in reverse.

Some of the bristles or spikes pierced his foot and he was poisoned and became mortally ill. He appealed for a drink from life-giving wine held in the king's golden cup, but the king refused. Some accounts say he asked for water and the king relenting and remembering their friendship went to get it. Then the king deliberately let it dribble through his fingers and on the third occasion Diarmaid died. Grainne was so distraught that she killed herself.

The golden cup was hurled into a lochan and the lovers were reputedly buried at the foot of Glen Beag along with their white hounds.

Other parts of Scotland also lay claim to this tale although not so prominently. They include Loch Nell and Glen Lonan in Argyll, Strathconan, Kintail, Glen Coe, Knapdale and Saddell, in Kintyre. But Glen Shee and Glen Beag have the major claim. There are also two magic wells or springs in the area, Tobar nam Feinne, The Fingalians' Well; and

Tobar Ossian, Ossian's Well. Glen Shee, the faery glen, is rich in Celtic tales.

These stories are fast disappearing from the glens and this is a great pity.

In Gleann Lichd, behind that striking mountain range – the Five Sisters of Kintail – Diarmaid was believed by people of that area to have died from the boar's spines. Local tales say that at his dying cry for water a spring burst forth, known as Tobar an Tuirc, the Boar's Well. Diarmaid is believed to be buried at Dùnan Diarmaid, on the shores of Loch Duich.

One lovely, green and blue late spring day I climbed Ben Loyal, in Sutherland, known as the Queen of Scottish Mountains because of its shapely four, great, granite peaks seen across the Kyle of Tongue, and found that it, too, had Diarmaid and Grainne links. On its steep north side there are sections of loose stones known as the Screes of the Tusks and tradition says Fingal (Fionn) killed the boar there and dragged it down the north face. The legend has clearly got out of focus here, possibly in nineteenth-century translations from Gaelic to English.

The River Spean, near Loch Laggan, passes some legend sites, including the River Gulbin, Clach Gulbin, and Lochan Turc linked to another local belief that Diarmaid and Grainne were buried there. North-west of Saddell, in Kintyre, lies Beinn an Tuirc, the Mountain of the Boar, which, according to tradition in that area, is reputedly the site of the boar hunt.

Lovely Glen Lonan, near Oban, has a standing stone close to the modern road which is reputed to mark where Diarmaid died and is buried. Beinn Tianavaig, on Skye, was originally called Guilbheinn and tradition has it that Diarmaid and Grainne are buried there with their hounds.

In Argyll, Sliabh Ghaoil is generally translated as 'mountain of love' and it was on its slopes – according to one version of the story – that the Fianna caught up with the fleeing lovers and made them return to the royal court. There are evidently links between this old tale and the classical myths of Adonis and Achilles' heel and yet they are also clearly Celtic in character.

Other 'boar hills' do not have a connection with the legend although they are sometimes described as such. For example, some hills with names like Ben Gulabin are not linked to the Diarmaid and Grainne story and may, indeed, derive from 'beak-shaped' or 'curlew/whimbrel hill', such as Ben Gullipen, close to the Menteith Hills, near Aberfoyle, Perthshire, or Beinn a' Ghuilbein, near Garve. The original Gaelic is *gulban*, a beak, and *guilbneach*, the curlew.

Romantic tradition has it that Clan Campbell gained the Lordship of Lochow through marriage to an O'Duine heiress and this ancient and much respected pedigree was responsible for the boar's head emblem appearing in their heraldry. The Campbells are known in some accounts as Sìol Dhiarmaid, the descendants of Diarmaid, the son of Duibhne (Doon).

CHAPTER ELEVEN

NOW READ ON . . .

Some hills have historic pedigrees. Beinn Achaladair, near Bridge of Orchy, in Perthshire, presents a shield-like prow on its north-eastern side overlooking the remains of the old pine woods of Crannach, and from that angle it is one of the most impressive mountains in the Highlands.

The name Achaladair derives from old Celtic for a settlement near a hard-water field. From the modern A82 Glen Coe road, as it rises and twists northwards over the Blackmount, the traveller can see why it has earned this name. There is an oasis of green fields amid miles of heather moor and high mountains.

The Fletchers built a tower-fortress at Achallader (the modern map spelling) but later lost it through the trickery of the expansionist policies of the Breadalbane Campbells. Beinn Achaladair has looked down on momentous events and it can tell yet another story, this time of relatively modern origin when one of the most puzzling mountain rescue searches in Highland history took place and in which an unknown occult medium sent mysterious letters to the searchers.

It is a well-researched event and I have had the pleasure of meeting one of the men involved in trying to unravel what actually happened. He was Mr Sandy Harrison, honorary president of the Scottish Mountaineering Club. A great enthusiast for the work of the National Trust for Scotland, sadly he died in 1988. He took part in the controversial search for a climber who died on Beinn Achaladair in March 1925. Mr Harrison was friendly with the late J.W. Herries, former chief reporter of *The Scotsman*, who had a strong interest in psychic matters and in the occult. He was at Achallader and Tyndrum during the events.

I also have the pleasure of knowing Archie McKerracher, of Dunblane, a historian and researcher, who built on earlier researches carried out by the late Alasdair Alpin MacGregor, writer and historian, who was a personal friend of J.W. Herries.

On the morning of Sunday, 22 March 1925, three young men set out from Inveroran Hotel, near Loch Tulla, to climb Beinn Achaladair. It is important to note that then the Glen Coe road ran close to Loch Tulla and that the modern road is now much nearer Achallader Farm. Formal mountain rescue teams did not exist then and annual accident statistics were not publicly promulgated in the way they are now. However, newspapers sometimes reported such events in great detail. The men were Archibald MacLay Thomson, Douglas Ewen and Alexander Lawson Henderson (who was 30).

They were reasonably equipped and carried ice-axes, but unlike most of today's winter mountaineers they did not have crampons. They had little or no experience of climbing in winter. Thomson was doing the climb as part of amassing enough experience to apply to join the Scottish Mountaineering Club. Alexander Henderson had done some mountaineering in Europe during holidays from his work with the Inland Revenue in Paisley.

They left the hotel at 5.30 a.m. and crossed a ford on the Water of Tulla close to Achallader Farm. They arrived at the railway line above the farm around 7.30 a.m.

The day was clear, but frosty, and they had been warned of ice on higher slopes. The three men decided to head up a broad snow gully on the western slopes, but were not the first, nor the last, mountaineers to find a direct line posing problems. They found the going hard and it is possible they encountered very hard snow which meant bouts of slow, step cutting. By 9.30 a.m., when they stopped for something to eat, they were only around 2,000 feet.

Henderson was feeling the cold and wandered around. At 10.30 he set off ten minutes ahead of his companions who, for a time, kept him in sight – another familiar mountaineering pattern. He bore to the left and his friends eventually lost sight of him behind rocks.

Thomson and Ewen were held up by more hard snow and took to iced rocks, another pattern from the days when crampons were not as common as now and when the points of stones sticking up through the ice could be precariously walked on.

The two men agreed they could not descend over that particular piece of ground and reached the summit cairn around 1.25 p.m. They could find no trace of Henderson, but were not initially unduly worried because it is very easy for a small group on a climb to take different ascent lines and to temporarily lose touch with one another.

As time passed they did become worried and Thomson was lowered on a rope over a cornice to see if he could spot Henderson. This was probably in the area of the west and north-west cliffs of Beinn Achaladair. They shouted his name and – a safety aid of the time – operated a hand siren.

Ben Achaladair has an intermediate peak, Meall Buidhe (the yellow mound) between it and the northern Munro mountain, Beinn a' Chreachain. It is no easy matter to descend from Beinn Achaladair towards Meall Buidhe in winter, but the two men did that. They found no footprints of their friend in the lower sections of the ridge.

They returned to the summit of Beinn Achaladair at 6 p.m., had an urgent discussion and then returned again to Meall Buidhe, this time climbing to the top of that hill. They could not find any sign of Henderson and with dark falling fast they decided to return to Achallader farm and raise the alarm.

They reached the farm around 8.40 p.m. and were given food by the farmer and his wife, Mr and Mrs Duncan Smith, and rested for a spell. The Smiths tried to persuade them to stay the night, but the two men thought their friend might have descended the hill and, by way of Auch Glen on the eastern and south side of Beinn Achaladair and its neighbours, Beinn an Dothaidh and Beinn Dorain, got down to the line of the old road or the railway and reached Tyndrum village. They had originally decided to end their mountaineering trip at Tyndrum where there was a hotel.

They left the farm at 10.35 p.m. and walked the 16 miles to the Royal Hotel, arriving there in a state of exhaustion at 3.45 on Monday morning, having covered 44 miles in 22½ hours.

The hotel proprietor, Robert Stewart, raised the alarm and a full-scale search for Henderson by stalkers, shepherds and farmers was organised for the next day. A telegram seeking help was sent to the Scottish Mountaineering Club offices in Edinburgh, but was not immediately seen and opened.

However, by Wednesday, groups of experienced SMC members arrived from Edinburgh and Glasgow and a 15-mile radius around the mountain was searched in conditions of snow, sleet and rain and which included some neighbouring peaks. The search was reported in newspapers.

Then events took a strange and supernatural turn.

On Thursday, 26 March, a letter postmarked Peterhead, but with no date, arrived at the Royal Hotel and addressed to a Mr Garrett. It was decided that this might be Mr Garrick, leader of one of the search parties and a lecturer at the Royal Technical College, Glasgow. It was a letter of two voices: one or more persons recounting events and a 'supernatural' voice giving information. To clarify matters I have italicised the 'scout' or medium's words. It read:

Dear Sir,

A friend and myself have, within the last three months, received startling proof of the accuracy of the information regarding unknown people, which we have received from a supernatural agency.

Yesterday (Tuesday, 24th) it occurred to us that we might be able to get useful information as to the wherabouts of the lost Mr Henderson, and at 12 noon we approached the usual source of our information, and requested that a 'scout' be sent out to get any information possible. [This word, 'scout', puzzled the readers]. In the evening (about 6.30 p.m.) we asked for news, and the undernoted is verbatim:

'*The answer is slow in coming but our messenger now reports that it is raining and one, I think his name is Cameron, is heading towards the col, where the man is lying. The snow is deep here, perhaps 20 feet, and it may be that Cameron is not sure of his feet and we cannot influence him sufficiently – it may be, I say three, some say six, weeks ere he be found. Jim says he is warm yet . . .*

Where may he be found? Can no directions be given?

'*Such information as I have is scant, but the news is that he is warm, and we are not led to think he is asleep. What do you say of Death – there is no Death . . .*

'Where is he?

The voice continues:

'*He has not yet passed, but his needs are worldly. It is a col. Ask one, I think his name is Cameron, where he was at four of the clock today. They are still searching, and we are trying to help.'*

Now we do not know a single member of the search party, but should there be among them one of the name of Cameron, that would be one point correct, indicating an intelligence of some kind behind our information. I would say that in all probability the whole of the information as to location of the spot for which you are searching is correct, and that the information should not be treated lightly. Neither my friend nor myself are spiritualists, but interested in investigating phenomena we do not pretend to understand. In view of the nature of the information, we feel conscience bound to pass it on – it can do no harm and may be useful.

The letter was signed 'Anxious To Help'.

It aroused both scorn and interest among the rescuers because a Mr Cameron had indeed been on the mountain at 4 p.m. on the Tuesday and it had been raining at the time.

A second and bigger search was organised for the weekend. The weather improved on Sunday, 29 March. A plane flew from Renfrew aerodrome over the area where over 70 rescuers were again scouring the slopes. Slate workers from Ballachulish had joined the stalkers and shepherds, but the searchers again drew a blank.

On the following Saturday a second letter arrived, postmarked 2 April and again it was from Peterhead. This time it was addressed to Robert Stewart, of the Royal Hotel, whose name by that time had appeared in the press although Cameron's had not. Two sketches were enclosed and the writer said that neither he nor his friend were acquainted with the Beinn Achaladair area so they could not say whether they were accurate or not or even which way they should be read.

The letter said:

They are reputed to have been drawn for us by the 'scout' sent to the spot and the following is his information:

'*Leave Loch Tulla and go along the road until you come to Ford, which lies between the castle and the Big House and go up to the corrie. You go east and climb the corrie on your right hand.'*

Asked if nothing could be done, we were told that there would be no hope until a thaw for recovery of the body . . .

It was signed 'Still Anxious To Help'.

A third letter arrived almost immediately, clarifying the reference as being the ford over the Water of Tulla.

The distance between the farmhouse at Achallader and the ruined castle tower is less than 100 yards, but there is a second ford, now bridged, to the east of Achallader where the now empty farmhouse of Barravourich stands.

The letter went on with more information from 'the voice':

'Follow the valley – some say corrie – to its source and at an altitude of 3,060 feet they will get as close as I can tell you at present.'

We asked for a sketch of the place, but our 'scout' was with the searcher called MacKlairen. You will know if one of that name is out.

For the second time in this mystery, the letters named a person actually on the search and whose name had not appeared in the press. One of the rescue leaders was a Captain MacLaren, from Connel Ferry, near Oban.

Then a fourth letter arrived, postmarked 3 April, and giving its time of writing as 9 p.m. It quoted the writer as having questioned 'the voice' and saying:

We have found a definite aid to the climbers. It is in the shape of a tin box. It is still visible. Has our letter to Garrett been opened?
'Yes, it has been opened by one of the name of MacKlairen.'

This information shook the searchers, many of whom had been sceptical about the letters because Captain MacLaren and Mr Garrick were together at the hotel when the letter arrived and Garrick asked Captain MacLaren to open it as he was busy – an impromptu and coincidental act which no one could have foreseen.

'But as to the box – some say tin. This they will find not one hundred yards from the spot.'

Can the box be seen?

'*It is near the Coire Achallander* [note the old spelling] *and if they are quick they will find it . . .*'

The stream of the corrie starting at Ford?

'*Yes, you will follow the corrie, or some say coire, and it goes to the bogland at the altitude already mentioned – 3,060 feet. Yes, it is a burn, though the word is new to me. I regret my gernadion* [note: possibly a word for messenger] *is no longer here: but from the report delivered, the news is on climbing the korrie, or I believe corrie. I noticed a box I think he called it, and a kloot of linen. The word of the gernadion is in Scots and represents box-mullie.*'

What is mullie?

'*I am sorry my Scots is so poor, it is new to me. The gernadion spoke of the box as a mull-lie, that is, a little mull. The contents of the box is linen and it is stiff with batter . . . To climb the corrie is easy – it is commonly used by – help me with this – Gillies – pronounced gilly . . . The snow fall increases and I fear that many little clues will be obliterated. One thing remains that it is about altitude 3,060 feet that the find will be made.*'

Sir Arthur Conan Doyle, best known as the creater and author of *Sherlock Holmes*, who was born in Edinburgh, was deeply interested in the supernatural. He investigated the Beinn Achaladair case. He thought the word 'gernadion' was the name of an elderly Greek who learned Scots from another spirit. Mull, of course, is a Scots word for a type of snuff box. The word 'linen' might refer to a map and 'batter' could be cardboard.

The fifth and last letter, again postmarked Peterhead, arrived on 7 April at the Royal Hotel. It read:

Dear Sir, I am sorry we have not much to give you but it may be of inter-est to the 'speculators' [note: a reference to the fact that the letters were now arousing widespread public interest and controversy]. 3 p.m. Sat.

'*I say they have read your letter and whilst laughing in their faces I should say it is not in their hearts – they say, what of this? who is this?*'

Sat., 9 p.m.

'*My last advice is to take the corrie at Achallander House . . . and at*

*altitudes given, and to the north you should encounter your object. There is a
dark stone ridge – I forget the technical name – at or near the spot.'*

Is there a precipice?

'*Yes it is a precipice. I think MacKlairen said heugh or kleugh . . .'*

Have they got the rough map I sent them?

'*Yes, they say it is a copy of a map.'*

Can they make anything of it?

'*Yes, it is quite intelligible to them.'*

[This discussion about the map possibly arose because some of the
searchers had copied the sketches and then read the tracings the wrong way
round.]

Mon., 4 p.m.

'*The letters have caused much comment and some heed is being paid.
Two of the company believe your good faith – one is called Walker. Stewart
says "I know no one in Peterhead."'*

[Note: this remark was indeed made by Stewart when he opened the fourth
letter because it claimed one of the letter writers knew him.]

The letter was signed 'Still Anxious to Help'.

Some of the searchers decided to follow the sketches and other clues as
everything else had failed. A final and larger search was organised for
Sunday, 13 April, three weeks after Henderson went missing.

In the afternoon, the farmer, Duncan Smith, found the body of
Alexander Henderson lying face down in a shallow slope in the north-west
corrie where the sketches had shown him – very roughly – to be.

This interpretation of Henderson's route would make sense because he
probably hoped to catch up with his friends on the lower ground, *en route*
to Tyndrum – again a not uncommon mountaineering pattern ('see you in
the glen then').

Henderson had no broken bones, but a wound on his forehead. It
would appear he had slipped and struck his head on a rock. He had
apparently slid downhill for 150 feet until stopped by a boulder. He was
precisely at 3060 ft, as the letters stated.

His rucksack was still on his back and contained a broken vacuum flask sticking through the fabric. Some of the searchers thought that this was the mull or box with a linen kloot.

However, the letters had emphasised that the small tin box was some distance from the body and contained stiff linen. If it contained a linen map, Henderson may have dropped it further up the hill where his axe was found, but no trace of it was ever found.

His body was carried down to Bridge of Orchy and then to his native Cupar, in Fife, for burial.

It is no surprise that this strange affair sparked off much talk and speculation, and ranging from ridicule to puzzlement.

Even allowing for newspaper publicity, there is no way the mysterious Peterhead letter writer could possibly have known all of the names or other details. They were to tell J.W. Herries that they had seen a copy of *The Oban Times* reporting the search, but only late in the search period.

A reporter from the old *Dundee Advertiser* eventually tracked the letter writer down to a man called Norman MacDiarmid, who was in his late thirties and who had lived at Killin, Perthshire, before the First World War. He had independent means and had purchased Buchan Ness Lodge at Boddam, in Aberdeenshire, in 1920 and he wrote articles on natural history for journals and magazines. He was known to be a recluse.

Norman MacDiarmid refused to answer questions about the letters, but he was directly involved. The reporter then traced a friend who agreed to speak, but anonymously, and who lived in Peterhead. They and other friends had started seances some months previously, but only for fun. They quickly realised that MacDiarmid had gifts as a medium which were previously unknown to him. On some occasions he would start writing backwards at great speed. They believed he was receiving messages from an unknown source of a spiritual nature.

On the night the first Achallader letter had been written by them, there had been a social gathering in the friend's house attended by his wife, daughter, two friends and MacDiarmid.

They had been chatting normally and MacDiarmid had been tinkering with a radio when he began to write backwards automatically and it was only after the writing was held to a mirror that they realised it might have something to do with the reported disappearance of Alexander Henderson on Beinn Achaladair.

MacDiarmid's friends copied the messages into the letters and sent them on in case they were of assistance.

They all then tried to help MacDiarmid get further information over the next three weeks of the search. There is little further information about Norman MacDiarmid, but he had several meetings with Herries. He is believed to have worked at Glasgow docks after the Second World War, returning each night to a cottage near Stirling. He was clearly shy and retiring, and refused all invitations to speak about his ability to receive spirit messages. He was interviewed by Herries who had copies of the letters and who returned the originals to the Royal Hotel. Herries was impressed by MacDiarmid and his integrity.

The original letters, alas, disappeared and were probably destroyed when the Royal Hotel burned down in 1931 and the proprietor, Robert Stewart – still mystified by the whole event – died two years later.

CHAPTER TWELVE

SLICING THE SWELLINGS

I thought I knew Knoydart well, having spent several holidays there including a memorable climb of Ladhar Bheinn on a day of storms when magnetic rocks sent the compass awry. We descended down the back of the hill, eventually arriving at Inverie, and then had to climb back over the Màm Barrisdale at night with four of us following one torch.

We got back to our base at Barrisdale just before the mainland rescue team was alerted – but it was a close-run thing. Ah well, experience is a collection of near misses as friend and writer Hamish Brown perceptively remarks.

Then I came across another reference which opened up a whole new field of interest. The words Màm Bharasdail leapt out at me from a piece of Gaelic text which, with the help of Gaels, I was trying to unravel.

This historic pass formed part of a charm formula which was widely used in past times – as were many other hills and passes called Màm. (In some places the word appears as *màn*.) Many are known to modern hillwalkers and mountaineers, including the Màm Ratagain, which links Loch Duich in Kintail with Glen Elg and the Kylerea route to Skye, and which is known to modern tourist drivers. The Mhàm Mhór Dhuirach, the great Mam of Jura, and the Mam Chlach Ard run through the Rough Bounds of Knoydart from the once well-populated glens of Dessary and Loch Arkaig-side in western Lochaber. Others are on drovers' routes, such as the Màm Chlachaig in Mull, which fell into disuse when the modern road was driven through the Gribun cliffs in 1851.

This old cure-charm was recorded in print by Alexander Carmichael. Its use is part of the complex tussle and the intricate merging that went on between the Celtic nature lore of the hill people and incoming Christianity. For example, the charm had to be performed on a Friday –

An Easter service held at dawn on the summit of Dumyat, at the west end of the Ochils – an ever-increasing practice on Scottish hills where Christian services have replaced the old pagan rituals of sun worship

Ben Ledi, above the town of Callander, was one of the best-known hill sites in Scotland for the Beltane celebrations. To mark the start of the Celtic new year sacred fires were lit and offerings made to those birds and animals which might attack flocks of cattle, sheep and goats

Glen Finglas in the Trossachs was considered to be a faery glen long ago; a place where Scottish kings hunted deer and malevolent beings harmed travellers

Ben Gulabin dominates the Spittal of Glen Shee – the faery glen – in Perthshire and was believed to be the lair of the wild boar which eventually killed the Celtic hero Diarmaid, who had fled to the hills with his lover, Grainne

The Paps of Jura, the breast-shaped mountains, seen from the island of Islay. The Paps were the haunt of witches who scored the hillside and, when the first snows lay on the peaks, the local people said it was the witches laying out their linen to dry

A miniature shieling in a Breadalbane glen which contains stones, shaped by the flow of burn or river water, which depict an old man, his wife and their children. The tiny shieling, symbolic of a real building and a real family, was believed to have the power to bring good luck. A passing hillwalker has put an apple inside as food for the family

The ancient hill pass of the Corrieyairack, the most famous of General Wade's military roads which linked Ruthven and Dalwhinnie with Fort Augustus. Legend has it that a phantom piper leads the ghosts of marching soldiers along the road

The summit of Quinag in Assynt, where the mountains were created by Norse gods

Mountaineer Fred Gordon, chief ranger with Gordon District Council, at Corrour bothy in the Lairig Ghru in the Cairngorms, where at least two mountaineers have had 'supernatural' experiences

Clachnaben, near Banchory, on the fringe of the Cairngorms, a granite rock tor in an area where the devil is reputed to have shaped the rocks

Winter at the crest of the Kirkton Pass, between Balquhidder and Glen Dochart in Perthshire, where two naturalists saw a mysterious hunter in ancient clothing and a hillwalker's dog showed signs of fright. The crag is Leum an Eireannach (of the Goat's Leap)

The twisting canyon of the Whangie, a curious rock formation sited between Drymen and Milngavie, close to the Campsies, is popular with rock climbers. The deep cleft was believed to have been cut out by witches or the devil

a link with the Christian belief of Good Friday when Christ was crucified.

The Gaelic term *màm* is applied to a hill or mountain pass which is shaped like a female breast. It is also applied to a swelling of the body, especially an armpit gland or in the crotch. The idea was to use the charm to switch the swelling from the human body to a mountain pass or hill of similar shape. Sometimes, when a swelling burst in the form of an ulcer, the users of the charm would conclude that it had clearly worked. An iron or steel implement was used in the charm because metal was believed to have supernatural qualities.

It was not unknown for people wanting to use this charm to be a long way from a *màm*, but the incantation worked if they had a picture of a shape in their mind which they knew well from living in some other area in past time. The essential ingredient was that they had had *living* experience of a *màm*. It was no good trying to conjure up some general picture purely out of the imagination.

Methods varied a little from place to place, but generally iron or steel was held close to the mouth and the first words of the charm were uttered. Knives, axes and sewing or darning needles were all used.

The blade was applied in a ritual fashion to the sore place forming the Sign of the Cross and sometimes dividing the sore into sections, but only figuratively, never cutting the flesh. The sections of the sore were generally of some number which had magical meaning, such as three, seven or nine, or a combination of numbers.

Sometimes two instruments would be laid in the shape of the Sign of the Cross on the sore. These were generally an axe and a darning needle. After each 'crossing' had been operated, the implement or implements were pointed at the mountain or pass which included the word *màm* and which could either be seen or was known to lie in a particular direction. There were 12 hills or passes called *màm* on the island of Mull alone so there was generally no shortage of suitable cure sites.

When the implement was pointed at a *màm*, sacred words were uttered which generally took a similar form. For example, in relation to the Màm an Sgriodain (the Màm of the Scree) the words would be: '*Seo air Màm an Sgriodain*' (This on the Màm of the Scree) and the sore or its properties would be transferred there or the transference would get under way.

In some areas, an axe was placed on the ulcer or swelling and a blessing or charm uttered in the name of the Trinity and then the axe was lifted and struck into a block of wood, often sited at a house door. The act was sometimes repeated in relation to the number of *màms* in an area. For example, Knoydart is reputed to have nine although some of the names have disappeared from maps or memories. If the ulcer or swelling did not subside then the rite was repeated.

Alexander Carmichael wrote that striking at the swellings was trying on the nerves of the watchers and the patient who knew that wounds or death might follow the axe not being stayed in its downward swipe. 'It is said that if the operation is successful, the swelling subsides as it proceeds.'

Other formulae survive from other areas, but the basic pattern was the same. It was not unknown for a person to gaze from the mainland towards islands or from one island to another until the appropriate *màms* had been identified on the horizon or fixed in the mind.

Some sources say that at the end of the incantations the axe was pointed at the ground and words uttered which signified the sting and pain of the swelling were in the earth and ground.

CHAPTER THIRTEEN

SPELL OF THE WILD

The snows of January and February do not readily bring spring to mind and the deer, forced down to the lower ground, look tired and ill-nourished, but the signs are there.

When going from south Loch Earn, in Perthshire, up Glen Vorlich, which is part of the old hill crossing – the Bealach Dearg (the red pass) – to where the town of Callander now stands, I saw in succession three birds which meant much to the people of long ago. From high up on the steep sides of Ben Vorlich came the familiar single 'cough' of a raven.

The raven is one of the early nesters, like the eagle, and was a special bird in Celtic and Norse lore. It signified death and was widely believed to smell out forthcoming carrion. An old Highland saying states: 'Nest at Candlemas, egg at Shrovetide, bird at Easter: if the raven have not these he has worse – that is, death.'

Many centuries ago the son of a Kintail chief received his first drink from the skull of a raven. Both the Celts and the Norse people believed the raven had occult powers and this drinking rite enabled the infant to understand the language of birds.

There is a Gaelic saying that if a raven is seen early in the morning then good fortune would attend the person that day . . . and I had a good day.

Further up the hillside I saw an eagle circling, *iolair* (pronounced yoo-ler). The hill people of past times believed the eagle was king of the birds and perhaps of all the birds in the world. Eagles could take on human form and act like avenging angels. By March, it is already nesting. The eagle was believed to be very old. A Gaelic proverb says 'as old as a Loch Treig eagle' and feathers from that area were greatly prized for arrows.

Loch Treig (pronounced traig), on the fringe of Lochaber, and well known to Munro bashers, is much larger nowadays than in past times and is a reservoir.

The third bird, one of many with special associations and surpassing most, was the ptarmigan, a favourite bird of many mountaineers and the name of a mountaineering club of which I have very fond memories.

This mountain grouse is generally only found above the 2,000 feet mark and its white, winter plumage, creaking-cork call and short, curving flight in the snow or in thick mist high up on the ridges is one of the most evocative experiences of the Scottish Highlands.

In summer its plumage loses much of its white colour. The ptarmigan is a master of camouflage and can sit tight on a nest when hillwalkers are close by.

The name ptarmigan derives from the Gaelic *tarmach*, meaning 'to be the source of' and it was believed that from this bird originated all feathered life. The addition of 'p' in the name is thought to be French.

In our scientific age it is sometimes difficult to fully appreciate that the life of hill peoples in Scotland was often a blend of the pagan and Christian attitudes towards the natural world, and the dividing line between human and animal was never firmly fixed.

It was often ecologically wise. Mallards are believed to be the birds of Mary, the mother of Christ, and children were taught to admire the mothering of chicks by the mallard and never to molest her.

Good and bad omens and signs abounded, both in birds and animals and sometimes this depended on whether the person had a reputation as a seer or had signs in dreams. The landscape lived and teemed with 'spirits', but they were not all malevolent or fearsome.

Lucky signs included the widgeon on the wing, the oystercatcher or the first stonechat seen on grass. But the first stonechat of the day on a rock or road, the carrion crow, the hooded crow, and the rook – especially if approaching – could be harmful.

A beast rising could be a good sign; going away could be bad. Seeing pigeons tended to be favourable. Seagulls, particularly black-headed gulls, were believed to be the spirits of good on earth; their black caps being worn to expiate sins. The grey or ringed plover singing near a house in the dusk could be a death song. A group of tree sparrows or meadow pipits seen singing could mean the death of a child because they were singing a requiem.

The oystercatcher, the *gille brìde* in Gaelic lore, the servant of St Bride, was clearly good because it had the form of a cross in its plumage and it was reputed to have hidden Christ from his enemies under seaweed. The crossbill had a twisted bill because it tore at the nails on the Cross and has the blood of the Saviour on its chest. The cuckoo was *eun sìth*, a faery bird. It was believed to have its home underground like the faeries and went there on midsummer day.

Butterflies were traditionally not harmed because they took the souls of the dead to heaven and the yellow butterfly was believed to bear the markings of the folds of Jesus's shroud.

Many believed the swan had powers of healing and to kill or injure one was unlucky. To hear wild swans on a Tuesday morning before a person had broken fast was a good omen and to see seven, or a multiple of seven, swans in flight ensured happiness for the equivalent number of years. It was also a bird of sorrow and regarded as the wondrous bird of the Otherworld.

Animals as gods, malevolent beings and companions appear in profusion in the lore of hill and glen, and stags, deer and fawns could all have magical qualities. They could take on human form. Deer sometimes belonged to the faeries, and human beings, thrown out by other human beings, could be suckled by the deer.

White deer occasionally appear in the hills and were greatly prized as having near-magical or sacred qualities. King James VI's forester at Windsor, John Scandoner, was sent to the Blackmount hills to see if a white hind which had been seen in the Corrie Bà could be captured. He was aided by the Breadalbane Campbells and got as far as the great and neighbouring Corrie an Easain – where he saw the hind – before the terrain and weather defeated him. He reported that capture was possible, but feared the hind would be harmed. The King gave orders that it was to go free and passed a law protecting it.

The sixteenth-century Gaelic poet and hunter, Dòmhnall Mac Fhionnlaigh nan Dàn (1550–1600), an outstanding bowman, is buried at that most evocative of Highland churches, Cille Choireil, near Roy Bridge, wrapped in the hide of the last stag he killed.

He was an expert slayer of wolves in the area between Loch Ossian, near Ben Alder, and Fersit, near Loch Treig. He chose the spot himself so the deer could crouch on his head and the little calves rest by his side. As well as killing the deer for food and hides, he firmly believed he had a personal and spiritual link with them.

One of the reasons for the three peaks on Beinn Alligin, in Torridon, the Horns of Alligin, being considered so special was that three-horned stags were thought to be supernatural beings. There is also probably a link with the Christian doctrine of the Trinity.

The mountain hare, too, was a common form for faeries or witches to take and there is always something slightly fey about these animals, almost human-like, in their glance back and their craning stances.

The wild-cat could be a sign of witchcraft, but not for those clans who had the cat as a badge, as with the great federation of clans, Clann Chattan. It was a mystical animal in nature lore. One word in Irish Gaelic, *puss*, has been borrowed into English as a pet name. Monstrous cats dwelt in caves and cats were sometimes slowly roasted alive to invoke the devil.

The wild boar had special, supernatural status and symbolised strength and courage. The hill called the Boar of Badenoch, *An Torc* in the original Gaelic, which overlooks the Drumochter Pass on the busy A9, is reputed to be the haunt of a spectre of a boar. Its neighbouring hill, the Sow of Atholl, is a modern name and replaced Meall an Dòbhraichean, hill of the watercress.

Seeing goats was a sign for delaying a journey. Wild goats, probably descendants of domestic goats, can be seen in some hill country, including parts of Kintail, the east shore of Loch Lomond and areas of the north-west.

Goats are making a bit of a comeback nowadays with farmers and other country dwellers, but we have a long way to go yet before we reach the numbers of past times in Scotland when they were much in demand for milk, meat, skins and to make sporrans.

The goat is commemorated in a number of mountain names, including Stob Ghabhar, in the Black Mount, and may have come originally to Scotland in Norse raids.

The devil was believed to be half-man, half-goat and it was a custom to take the goat into the house of an ill person to take away infection. They frightened elves and goblins, and killed adders.

CHAPTER FOURTEEN

THE SNOWBALL SUMMER

One can look a bit of a fool wearing lady's red-diamanté, angled, sunglasses, but the need for them was dire. Some years ago a friend and I did a traverse of all the peaks, except the first, of that fine mountain, Ben Cruachan, and on a day of blazing sun.

I was a novice and ill-equipped – no hat and no sun spectacles. At the end of the day I had a splitting headache and felt sick, sure signs of minor heat or sun stroke. What saved me from more severe repercussions was that we found long, snow banks in the gullies on the north side of the mountain and I crammed snow down my neck and rubbed my head and arms with it.

We headed for the village of Taynuilt the next day and I bought the last pair of sunglasses they had in the shop. They looked bizarre on me and I got many a strange glance, but they were functional.

Snow on Ben Cruachan in summer stuck in the mind and I was intrigued to find out in later years that the snow had a symbolic importance and that the Clan MacIntyre, who lived on Loch Etive-side and in Glen Noe ('the new glen'), paid their annual rent to the Campbells of Inverawe by means of a snowball taken from the corries of Ben Cruachan in midsummer.

This was regarded as a ceremony of major importance and was a custom also followed by the MacSorleys of Glen Nevis in relation to Clan Cameron, by the tenants of the Grants of Rothiemurchus who went to the Cairngorms for snow (an easy task), and the Foulis who did the same on Ben Wyvis (rather harder).

Strictly speaking, the snowball was not the actual rent, particularly as time went on. The MacIntyres paid rent in the normal way of supplying men-at-arms, or money, or in cattle or meal. The snowball was the symbol of their tenure on that spot, of security, of their desire to be there. The MacIntyres' tradition may have its roots in heroic Celtic saga and legend.

The original name of the MacIntyres in Gaelic was *Mac an t-Saoir*, Son of the Carpenter. They had a tradition that Olaf the Red, Norse King of the island of Man, and Somerled, Thane of Argyll, had a quarrel when their galleys were sailing on the same raiding foray. Olaf had turned Somerled down when he wanted to marry Olaf's daughter.

Somerled's nephew, Maurice MacNiall, was in Olaf's galley and secretly bored holes in the hull when the two craft lay at anchor. He covered the holes with tallow and butter. When they sailed from Skye to Ardnamurchan, Olaf's galley began to sink. He called to Somerled for help. Somerled said he would only assist if he got to marry Olaf's daughter and, because he was in such peril, Olaf agreed. Somerled hauled him aboard his own galley. When Olaf could no longer see what was happening with his own ship, Maurice MacNiall plugged the holes with pins he had already shaped and the galley was saved.

From then on Maurice MacNiall was known as *An Saor*, the Carpenter, and his descendants as *Mac an t-Saoir*, Son of the Carpenter.

The clan's original home was on the islands. Some authorities say Skye, others Islay, but six centuries ago they decided to go walk-about. They approached Ben Cruachan from the south-west – which would favour the Islay tradition – driving their cattle and carrying their weapons and goods with them. As well as housing a witch who was reputed to haunt Ben Cruachan (see page 85) they believed that the mountain contained a living spirit which spoke to them.

It guided them as to which pass they should take and said that they should make their new home where the White Cow in their herd, which was revered as having a supernatural nature, should lie down after crossing the Lairig Noe (or *Nodha*, in Gaelic) which runs from the B8077 road north of Dalmally and close to Castles Farm and then over to the shores of Loch Etive. This pass runs between the eastern outliers of Ben Cruachan and these two striking mountains, Beinn a' Cochuill and Ben Eunaich.

The White Cow stopped about half a mile from the shores of Loch Etive in Glen Noe and the MacIntyres found much of the area pleasantly wooded and with good grazing. It was there they settled for over five centuries.

An old Gaelic saying states that the two oldest farmers in Alba (Scotland) are the farmers of the apple tree which grows on the shores of Loch Etive and the MacIntyres of Glen Noe.

They became foresters (or deer managers) to the Stewarts and then to the Campbells of Glen Orchy and Breadalbane. Some did not always like Campbell overlordship and fought with Montrose's army in the seventeenth-century Scottish Wars of the Covenant and in the Jacobite Risings.

The snow which paid their symbolic rent at midsummer to the Campbells was taken from *Coir' an t-Sneachda*, the Snowy Corrie of Ben Cruachan, and a white calf was also handed over. In their herd they had at least one white cow so when a white calf was born it was a matter for rejoicing.

They gathered at a flat stone, now split in two by ice and water action, upon which they held a midsummer barbecue. The stone, the *Clach an Laoigh Bhiata*, the Stone of the Fatted Calf, can still be seen and is passed by many hillwalkers unaware of its significance. It stands about two feet high and lies just below the crest of the pass on the south side with a little burn, and former well, close by. To the east lies a line of old poles put up to mark the line over the crest.

The calf was killed beside this stone and then was cooked and eaten by the MacIntyres and the Campbells.

The small well, now overgrown, was called *Tobar na Feusaig*, Well of the Beard or Whiskers, because of the grasses growing alongside.

At one time the snowball and the fatted calf were sufficient as symbolic rental, but money eventually came into it and the Campbells gradually increased the rent until, in 1806, the last MacIntyre chief gave up his tenancy of Glen Noe.

The chief's house, known as *Larach na Bà' Bàine*, or Habitation of the White Cow, once stood on the side of Loch Etive, and not far from the modern farm the Clan MacIntyre Society has erected a memorial cairn.

It is worth visiting the old priory at Ardchattan, on the shores of Loch Etive, not far from the Connell road, and where some of the MacIntyre chiefs are buried. On one of the gravestones, dated 1695, is a round object, like a heraldic orb, but which may, in fact, commemorate the snowball rent.

Above Dalmally stands the monument to one of the best-known MacIntyres, Duncan Ban, Fair Duncan of the Songs, whose Gaelic nature and love poems still live on and can be read in modern English translations. It was erected in 1859.

CHAPTER FIFTEEN

BATTLE OF THE BULL

Diana's ghost is reputed to haunt the hills to this day and some walkers claim to have seen a ghostly figure in the mist.

Diana died because she could not run fast enough. She also met her bloody fate because she had an eye for a tasty morsel.

High on the crest of the old bealach (pass) linking the deep-cut sea loch and soaring green and brown mountains of Torridon with the golden beaches and green coastline of Gairloch, a little cairn was built in memory of Diana. It is called Carn Dioneig on the large-scale map but has vanished from the Ordnance Survey metric sheets and from guidebooks – a sign of a cultural decline in those mapping or writing about the ancient traditions of the western Highlands.

A group of us went looking for the cairn one glorious day of bright sunshine when the rocks of Torridon, among the oldest in Britain, glistened in the sun; when little blue lochans winked on the tawny moors and when that evocative sound of a Highland spring and early summer, the voice of the cuckoo, was heard in the glens.

We were on a trek round Beinn Alligin, the jewel-mountain, one of Torridon's most ascended hills and which has had more deaths and injuries on it than its spectacular steep-sided, cliff and buttress neighbour, Liathach, the grey one.

The path uphill into Coire Mhic Nobuil beside the chuckling burn was a delight, with brown pools inviting a paddle or swim and the big hills striped like tigers with the remains of spring snow clinging on in the gullies.

The moor grass and heather is besprinkled with many boulders and the great boiler plates of rock have dozens of isolated stones perched on them – the result of many years of storm and ice action. Sometimes it is easy to spot a cairn. In Diana's case, prominent stones were sticking up all over the place.

In the dim past and at Christmas time, 12 men from Gairloch came over the pass on their way to Loch Carron to see what they could find to add to their festive supplies. By coincidence, they met 12 men from Loch Carron *en route* to Gairloch and they had a woman, Diana, with them.

The first party got nothing, but the Loch Carron men obtained a bull. They drove it through the pass and rested at a knoll beside Loch a' Bhealaich, loch of the pass, sometimes called Meall an Tairbh or knoll of the bull.

By coincidence they met the empty-handed party and, after discussion, the two groups decided to divide the bull between them. It was slain and in the process of being cut up when they discovered that the tasty fat or suet (some accounts say the liver) was missing and someone in the company was concealing it. They may have been drinking because an argument broke out which led to weapons being drawn and then a full-scale battle took place.

The ground was strewn with dead or wounded men and when the sole survivor, a Gairloch man, looked around he initially assumed everyone else was a casualty.

Then he saw a solitary figure running away towards Torridon through the gap between Beinn Alligin and its neighbour to the east, Beinn Dearg (pronounced jerrak, the red mountain). It was Diana, allegedly clutching her spoils.

He ran after her and finally caught up with her at the crest of the pass. Without compunction, he slew her. Her friends and relatives later found her body and erected the cairn.

We sat down on a sunny rock and contemplated the scene. It was startling to think of such a horrendous deed in such a beautiful place.

Not far from Loch Toll nam Biast, loch of the beast's hollow, on the north-east side of Beinn Alligin, we found a low cairn, with an ancient look, with large and moss-covered stones. It overlooked the scene of the brawl and the route a fugitive would take.

CHAPTER SIXTEEN

FEARS, FROLICS, FAERIES

On the steep, green slopes of the Ochils above the small village of Menstrie stands a little knoll of a hill called Craigomas. Because it stood at the mouth of Menstrie Glen and was easily reached, parts of it were a playground for generations of children.

I first went up it when I was six or seven and with my brothers and sisters was enchanted to find that it had a faery ring – a distinct circle in the grass in a little hollow on the northern side. The circle was, of course, caused by a pattern of grasses or by frost and ice action, but the name faery ring stuck and I have often gone there to show it to the young children of friends.

The faery ring has gone now, probably for ever. A bulldozed farm track was in recent times cut up the hillside, fringing Craigomas. It initially followed an older 'road' constructed to bring calcite down from a mine on Myreton Hill, and then ran back along the side of Menstrie Glen. It altered the drainage pattern and the faery ring disappeared.

The bulldozed track close to the sides of Craigomas is in marked contrast to the attitude of older generations who would not take wood, soil or peat from a faery mound, believing that the souls of their predecessors dwelt there. Belief in faeries influenced people from Barra to the Borders.

They had a practical link with the faery world, not just pretty-pretty stories, and the roots of faery belief may lie with the vanished race – the small, dark men who possessed the land before history and who were pushed back into hill recesses by stronger invaders. The widely held belief that faeries fear cold iron may have links with Bronze Age peoples being defeated by Iron Age peoples.

One of the reasons why faeries carried off mortal children was in the hope that they would rear one who would be their leader and not fear cold iron. They hoped to drive out the mortals who had stolen the land from them. Fear of the faeries stealing a child and leaving a changeling was very real.

The faeries were practical and handsome people and carried shields and weapons which were often jewel-encrusted. They had pipers and fiddlers and were accompanied by faery dogs who had green coats and golden eyes. Their dwelling places, their pleasure domes, were conical-shaped mounds and hills which are plentiful in Scotland.

The ancient gods, driven underground below the hills, were relegated in folk memories to faeries, the people of the hills.

The faeries were sometimes called *Sluagh Fhionnlaidh*, Finlay's People, after the name of their reputed chief, although there is a strong Cairngorms tradition that the King of the Faeries was *Dòmhnall Mòr Bad an t-Sìthein*, who lived near Loch Morlich, in Glen More, and two small hills, the *sìthean* or faery mounds which are traditionally linked to him, can be seen.

Our hill world is peppered with knolls, hills and mountains with faery associations. There was hardly a parish in Scotland which did not have a faery knowe but these are gradually – and sadly – being forgotten.

In every region there was a larger or more prominent hill where the faeries gathered and held rallies and what seemed to be policy conferences. They included Tom-na-hurich, in Inverness; Doon Hill or the Faery Hill of Aberfoyle; Calton Hill, in Edinburgh; and the Eildons in the Borders.

On a recent hill-tramping visit to Mull and neighbouring Iona and by an initial scanning of the map sheets I logged at least six faery hill or loch names on Mull alone and another three on Iona. This pattern can be repeated all over the Scottish hill world.

The mounds were known as *sìthean*, which is often given as shian, or as cnocan, little knolls. At Halloween between sunset and sunrise it was possible for human beings to gain entrance to a faery shian. At that time the faeries often moved house so it was the best time to mount a rescue operation to take back any mortal who may have been stolen.

The precise sitings of many of these stories are being lost. In Glen Quey, an old Ochils cattle route between Castle Campbell, at Dollar, and Glen Devon, there is a little well to the south side of the path called the Maiden's Well. Who she was is now obscure, but a local tradition has it that any traveller falling asleep beside the well will wake up in faeryland. There is also said to be a faery knowe nearby which contains a phantom piper, but no one now seems to know the 'authentic' version of this story or where the knowe is sited. This is fast becoming a saddening trend.

The faeries lived all over Scotland – beneath the grassy slopes of Ceann a' Bharra, on the island of Barra, in the Outer Hebrides; on Cairnsmore of Carsphairn, in Galloway; on Beinn Iadain, in Morvern; in Glen Shee (Gleann Sìthe, the faery glen); on Ben Tee, in Lochaber; on Ben Shee, in the Ochils; on Beinn Shian, at Strathyre, in Perthshire; in Glen Feshie, which was particularly popular; on flat-topped MacLeod's Tables, Healaval Mór and Healaval Beag, on the island of Skye, whose inner recesses held treasure and where the faeries were 1,000 years old; on Beinn Hiant (Shianta), the charmed or faery hill in Ardnamurchan; in hillocks between Opinan and Diabaig, in Torridon, where people heard faery music, and Borders hills like Broad Law, the highest hill of the the Manor group, near Tweedsmuir, or the hills of Teviotdale . . .

The faeries chose these mainly conical shaped or grassy-sloped mounds because they didn't like corners. The cuckoo, a faery bird like the corncrake, was believed to go inside such mounds and not migrate. It emerged again in the spring to announce the start of the golden days of sunshine and warmth.

The faeries had the power known as the *fith-fath* (sometimes given as fath fith, pronounced fee-fawh) – the power to change someone into some other creature, such as a hare, a deer or a seal, while still keeping their own personality. People long ago took such powers very seriously and elaborate ceremonies were carried out to ensure an unbaptised infant was not taken away.

The faeries could affect health, the state of cattle, cause storms, influence fishing and hunting. You had to keep on the good side of the faeries. If you did that, then you were all right. They were often known – in benevolent mood – as the People of Quietness and the word *sìth* also means peace. But caution was needed. The word *ban-sìth*, faery woman, gives us the modern word banshee.

In some parts of the Highlands some elderly people will still put out a gift for the faeries although this practice is dying fast, but I know one (unnamed and embarrassed) stalker who still does that from time to time beside a faery mound.

Their powers were not unlimited: like witches, the faeries or faery beasts could not cross running water and there may be an ancient link here with some burns or rivers being – like the hawthown – a land boundary marker in past times.

Beinn Dorain, at Bridge of Orchy, that lovely, sweeping, cone-shaped mountain so beloved of Gaelic poet Duncan Ban Macintyre, was also a haunt of faeries.

The most prominent of all the faery hills is soaring and prominent Schiehallion, whose cone shape dominates Loch Rannoch and which appears in so many postcards and calendars. In Gaelic it was *Sidh Chailleann* – the Faery Hill of the Caledonians. At 1,083m, it is the highest of the faery hills.

The MacGregors of Rannoch-side took stone slabs from its slopes as gravestones, partly because the stone was suitable for such a purpose and partly because of the 'special hill' status attached to stones taken from such a place.

The word Caledonian is a Roman term, but the name may derive from old Gaelic or Celtic for a wooded stronghold.

Professor William MacGillivray, the Aberdeen naturalist, reported in 1850 that he had interviewed a man who had seen faeries dancing on a hillock, called the Faery Knowe, on the Tolmount pass, the famous crossing over the Mounth from the Angus glens to Deeside. The man had sworn that the faeries had a piper.

James Hogg, the Ettrick Shepherd, interviewed the last man to see the faeries in the Forests of Yarrow and he gave us much detail.

Green was the special colour of the hill faeries.

A gravel road leads from Glenmore Lodge in the Cairngorms, through the Ryvoan Pass to Abernethy. In the middle is beautiful Lochan Uaine (pronounced oo-an-yeh) or the green lochan, well known to generations of mountaineers. An old legend says the faeries wash their clothes in it. Scientists say that rock particles are suspended in the water and cause light to be reflected. The loch is fed and drained underground. The water stays clear and fallen trees at the bottom of the loch can be easily seen.

Coire Lagan, in the Cuillin of Skye, also has a green lochan although the water is sometimes tinged with green and does not have the impact of

Lochan Uaine. The faeries were also reputed to clean their green garments in it.

Skye female faeries traditionally wore green, but the men were called little red fellows, *na daoine beaga ruadh*, and were clad in garments dyed a crotal or warm brown colour, the dye coming from lichen on the rocks. They sometimes had blue bonnets. Mull faeries were reputed to have one nostril although the reason is not known.

In the Southern Highlands, between the Munro-mountains of Ben Ime and Ben Vane, there is a tributary of the Inveruglas Water, known as the Allt Coire Grogain, which receives other burns. Near the head of this glen is Lag Uaine, the Green Hollow, which had a faery pool where the faeries of Lennox had a dye factory for their clothing.

Sir Walter Scott, who wrote the epic poem *The Lady of the Lake* in 1810, knew the Trossachs area very well and, in particular, Glen Finlas. He wrote in a note to the poem that the glen's name could translate as the Glen of the Green Women and pointed out that although green was the colour of the faeries it was considered an unlucky colour in some other parts of Scotland.

The Trossachs are rich in faery lore.

The east side of Ben Venue overlooking Loch Katrine has the famous Coire nan Uruisgean, a meeting place for all the uruisks or faery-demons in Scotland. It is situated among the deep boulders which lie just above the Bealach nam Bo, the route the MacGregors used for their cattle raids into the Lowlands, and can be clearly seen by climbers on Ben A'n on the other side of the loch.

Strictly speaking the uruisk (Gaelic, *ùruisg*) was half-man, half-goat, but of the faery race. Several modern books refer to them as goblins. One of them haunted Beinn Dorain, but was banished by St Fillan and the incoming new faith of Christianity. Others lived near Glen Orchy, in Argyll, near Loch Sloy, at Loch Lomond-side, in parts of Lochaber and the Skye Cuillin. Breadalbane was a very popular area for uruisks. The faeries had an affinity with the red deer of the hills and, earlier, with the reindeer which were in Scotland until the beginning of the thirteenth century and probably later. The faeries milked the deer, a practice which still goes on with the Lapp races of Northern Norway, Sweden and Finland, and their great herds of deer.

Faery cows once roamed the pastures of Ben Lawers, in Tayside. They were dun coloured and hornless. They used to get with calf in a way that mystified local people until they were seen on the fringes of Loch Tay, where they stood lowing for a supernatural water bull which inhabited the loch.

CHAPTER SEVENTEEN

MAGIC MAKES THREE

The three peaks of the prominent Eildons are among the most photo-graphed views in Scotland. They lie close to historic Melrose in the heart of Sir Walter Scott country and were part of Sir Walter's favourite view.

These striking hills reach to 1,385ft (422m) and the three peaks gave their name to the major Roman fort of Trimontium which was built at Newstead, near Melrose. The northern hill housed a fortified town built by local tribes which contained 300 houses.

It is a pastoral landscape, but once upon a time the Eildons rose out of a wilder landscape, of bog and marsh and thick forests, and the people of the area looked to them for refuge and as a sacred place. Sun worship was carried out there.

In legend the shape of the Eildons was put down to the devil cleaving the range into three on the challenge of a local wizard, Michael Scott, whose pedigree is shadowy.

Born around 1160 AD, he died in 1235. He may not even have been born in Scotland and is said to have studied at Oxford, Paris and Padua and to have visited Bologna and Rome. He is known to have been in Toledo, Spain, in 1217. He translated the works of Aristotle and is reputed to have known the Emperor Frederick.

The roots of the wizard tale might be no more than puzzlement over a scholar's intense and single-minded attachment to documents and 'inexplicable' and lengthy sojourns abroad.

Sir Walter Scott was responsible for giving the legend prominence. The devil had originally intended to misbehave elsewhere and his idle hands were directed to splitting the Eildons.

The hills are also linked to another supernatural event, the kidnapping of 'Thomas the Rhymer' who spent seven years in faeryland. Sir Walter

Scott gave the time as 12 years. It is virtually impossible to disentangle fact from fiction in his case.

Thomas the Rhymer may have been Thomas Lermont, or Learmont, of Ercildoune (now Earlston), who probably lived from about 1220 to 1297. The story told in ballad form says he encountered the Queen of the Faeries at Huntleybank, near Melrose, and there is still a Rhymer's Glen to the south-west of Huntleybank.

The Queen led Thomas below the Eildons and later restored him to earth but told him she would summon him again. She gave him the power of prophecy and he was reputed to make these from the shade of the Eildon Tree – a site marked by a stone at the side of the A6091 road. The stone was erected in 1929.

Sir Walter Scott refers to an earlier stone in notes to the ballad in his *Minstrelsy of the Scottish Border*. There is a Bogle burn and a Goblin brook nearby.

The legendary King Arthur and his Knights are said to rest beneath the Eildons and wait for the hour when they will be called upon to save his country. Arthur is the most famous of the Celtic mythological figures and yet was a real person living in the fifth and early sixth centuries AD.

By medieval times he and his warriors had become firmly embedded in mythology and the later Arthurian tales bear a strong resemblance to many Celtic stories of Fionn Mac Cumhail and his warriors, the Fianna.

Merlin, the magician of Arthurian legend, is reputed to have been buried near Drumelzier, on the B712, outside Peebles. The knoll on which Drumelzier church stands is pointed out as the site.

He was a magician or druid who played an important part in the sagas. He was clearly Celtic in origin and his name was originally given as Myrddin. However, it was widely believed that the ghost of Merlin still stalks the Borders hills, perhaps in the guise of a hart.

Broad Law, at 2,775ft (839m) – the highest summit in the Manor group and within ten feet of the height of The Merrick, the highest point in southern Scotland – has a spring on its side beside which Merlin was fond of reclining. Hart Fell, in the Moffat Hills, was also reputed to be his home.

CHAPTER EIGHTEEN

WEATHER AND WITCHES

Ben Cruachan, above Loch Awe, in Argyll, is nowadays a popular, two-Munros mountain whose twin peaks (sometimes three) draw the eye from so many other hills.

But it is surely not its statistics that make it special? They are, indeed, impressive although there are 28 other mountains in Scotland bigger than it. It has eight main tops, and towers above mid Lorn like some huge dun or fortress, and its massif extends to almost 20 square miles.

My own first acquaintance with it came before 1965 when the North of Scotland Hydro Electric Board (now Scottish Power) placed a large dam in the main, southern corrie as part of a £24.5 million scheme. The first large-scale pumped storage development in Scotland also meant constructing a cavern inside the mountain as big as a seven-storey building.

Yes, I know it is necessary and that power from the glens is relatively cheap once the dams, pipes and buildings have been constructed. And I realise that care has been taken with appearance and to minimise, not always successfully, environmental damage. But Ben Cruachan is a giant, and I fear the giant some of us knew has been slain.

It was always a Celtic mountain. From the old, hilltop fort at Dunadd, near the modern Crinan Canal, the cradle of Scotland, white-clad kings and lords reputedly placed their foot in a carved niche and looked to the twin prongs of *Cruachan Beann* (pronounced Croo'ahun B'youwn) and made their vows to serve and rule with courage and compassion.

An old tale says that the Cailleach Bheur, the witch of the storms, also had homes on Ben Nevis, Beinn a' Bheithir at Ballachulish, at Morrone, near Braemar. She was one of the best known mountain witches and when she made a leap from Ben Cruachan to Dunadd she left the famous footprint mark on Dunadd's rock.

High in a secret corrie on the mountain lay the ancient Well of Youth, guarded by the Cailleach Bheur who preserved her beauty by bathing each evening in its waters.

But one night, after herding her goats across stepping stones at Loch Etive, she fell asleep and forgot to put the capstone on the little spring so that it gushed all night down the mountain and in the morning the 20 miles of Loch Awe lay at its foot.

The witch grew ugly, old and vengeful and next time you are being battered by sleet and screeching winds on the mountain it is her icy and screaming voice which you'll hear. There's a scientific explanation for Loch Awe as well, but it is much more dull.

The Cailleach Bheur drove her favourite cow from its byre on the Mull of Kintyre to the summit of Ben Cruachan where it drank from a magic well. She was so tall she could wade across the Sound of Mull no more than knee deep, and the smaller islands were formed from the earth and stones which spilled from the creel she was carrying. Another legend says the hills of Ross-shire were formed the same way.

The Cailleach Bheur is sometimes described as having a refuge on Beinn a' Bheithir, pronounced *vair*, at Ballachulish, to the west of Glen Coe – a word which can also mean serpent or lightning.

She haunted dark caves and mountain corries. She was venomous and destructive, and her reputation may have been mixed up with another tale of a dragon that lived on Beinn a' Bheithir and killed unwary travellers.

Ben Vair was long ago known as Ben Gulbin, a name linked to the story of the runaway lovers, Diarmaid and Grainne, the pursuing Fianna and the legendary magic wild boar (see page 50).

The Cailleach Bheur's chief seat was on Ben Nevis and she kept a beautiful maiden a prisoner there. Her son fell in love with the maiden and they eloped and she pursued them in vain creating fearsome storms in her anger and fury. Traditionally, 25 March was considered to be *Latha na Cailliche* when a cold wind could blow for days.

There can be understandable confusion over the different Highland witches and some sources say three main ones are all the same evil hag, but they would appear to be separate beings.

The Cailleach Bheur had a twin sister, A' Mhuilearlach, who was responsible for storms at sea.

Strictly speaking, the Cailleach Bheinn a' Bhric, another of the brood who lived mainly around Loch Ossian and Loch Treig, on the fringe of Lochaber, was not a witch as such, but a spirit.

Another famous witch, the witch of Moy, Gormshuil, who frequently comes into clan legend, seems to have stayed clear of the hills.

The activities of the Cailleach Bheur and her sister-witches became deeply lodged in Highland and Lowland folklore.

Sacrificial rites were carried out at Beltane which were intended to mean her death as the warm days of spring and summer approached. She was sometimes the theme of a dance at harvest home, called the Cailleach of the Quern-Dust, and her name was often given to the last sheaf of corn from the first field reaped in harvest – an object of communal scorn. Her name was also given to a piece of twisted wood brought home from the glens or peat-bogs and burned on Christmas Eve on top of the peat fire, thus ensuring a year without harm.

The witches could transform themselves into animals, particularly hares, cats or hill birds, and it was the custom in the Highlands to break egg shells so that the witches could not use them for boats. They could make cattle ill, wreck crops, harm the fishing, or bring disaster on armies.

Witches' sites are all over Scotland's hills and this is particularly true of the Cailleach Bheur. She kept her cattle in rocks above Gorten, in Ardnamurchan, *Bàthach na Cailliche* – the Witch's Byre. She herded deer in Glen Nevis. She and friends washed their linen in the Gulf of Corrievreckan, between Scarba and Jura, in Argyll, and when the 'whirlpool' thrashed white and roared in storms, their linen was being thoroughly washed and they had put on their kerchief or 'hat', their whitest garment. When the first snows lay on the Paps of Jura, it was the witches' linen being spread out to dry. The tidal race is known as the Cailleach. The name Corrievreckan may not derive from the old legend of Prince Brecan, who was allegedly drowned in the Gulf, but may, in fact, mean the cauldron of the tartan or plaid, from the Gaelic word for tartan, *breacan*.

Scrapes like plough-marks on Schiehallion, the faery hill of the Caledonians, in Perthshire, have been attributed to her claws, and Beinn an Oir (the Mountain of Gold) on the island of Jura has Sgriob na Cailliche, or the Hag's Scrape, on its sides, where the witch clawed the hillside in the fury of the storms.

The name Mountain of the Gold may take its name from iron pyrites found there and on the neighbouring island of Islay, but faery-gold was also used to describe such terrain and this might have added to the hill's supernatural status. Beinn Shiant, the most northerly of the three Paps – a wonderful day's traverse – translates as the sacred, consecrated or enchanted mountain.

Witches' sites are all over our hills. Many are linked to terrain which is frightening or oppressive, deep corries, dark glens, little ravines, gloomy crags. This is particularly true of witches' sites in the Ochils where nearly all are linked to dark corners in otherwise open, sunny, grass and heather hills. An exception is Ben Donich, in the Arrochar hills, a name which can translate as evil or vile, yet it generally seems a light and sunny corner.

Not all hills called *cailleach* necessarily mean a witch, but the Scots word carlin generally does. The rocky ridges of Arran have *Ceum na Caillich*, the Carlin's Leap or Witch's Step. The rocky gap at the Slacks of Glencarvie, in the Braes o' Mar, was known in the past as *Sloc Cailliche* after the witch the Cailleach Bheathrach, who bit out the sloc with her teeth while trying to cut a way through for the water on the Don side to flow into the Dee.

In many parts of the country people point to a Witches Knowe or Gallows Hill where witches were executed or to cliffs, such as Witches Craig, above Logie, near Stirling, or the Knock of Alves, near Forres, in Moray, where the covens were reputed to meet. Dark pools in burns were often known as the witches' linns, such as Talla Linn, near Broad Law, in the Southern Uplands.

Witches' anecdotes were strong in the Borders hills, particularly in Teviotdale. Odd rock formations, such as the rock pillar, Carlin Maggie, in the Fife Lomonds, often got witches' names. The striking peaks of the Five Sisters of Kintail, in the north-west, were said to have been created by a shadowy warlock.

Legend tells how seven beautiful princesses lived close to Loch Duich. One night a ship was wrecked on the shore and the local ruler assisted its owners – two tall, blond princes – to refurbish their vessel and the seven maidens all fell in love with them.

When the time came for them to set sail, they asked the king if they might marry his two youngest daughters, promising that their five, older, and just as handsome and rich brothers would come to court the remaining sisters.

The king agreed and the two brides sailed away with their lovers and were never seen again. The brothers never came.

The princesses agreed with one another that they would wait for ever so the Grey Magician took pity on them and turned them into mountains where they could wait and watch for the ship that never comes.

Worship of the gods also took place on mountain tops. There are arguments over the meaning of Ben Loyal, in Sutherland, but it may derive from the Norse, *laga fjall*, the law mountain. People sometimes gathered on such hills in Norse areas to hear legal judgements and proclamations. Altars to the god Thor, for example, were built there.

CHAPTER NINETEEN

PERILS AND PROTECTION

There are a lot of Beinn Bhreacs, or dappled hills, in the Highlands. The name is sometimes given as Bhric or Breck, as in Robert Louis Stevenson's hero in the novel *Kidnapped*, Alan Breck, who had a pock-marked face.

The most famous Beinn Bhreac or Beinn a' Bhreak (given on modern maps as Beinn a' Bhric) lies to the south-west of Loch Ossian, north of the Blackwater reservoir, and about three miles south-west of Corrour rail halt on the West Highland line. It was home to an extremely powerful and well-known witch.

Once, when I was staying in the most evocative and best of youth hostels, that wooden shelter at the south end of Loch Ossian, I changed plans, borrowed an ice-axe from the much-liked warden, Tom Rigg, and set off for Beinn a' Bhric.

The day became foul – huge squalls of rain, sleet and high winds – and I grinned wryly at the thought of the witch or carlin of Beinn a' Bhric, Cailleach na Beinne, making life hard for me.

I was looking for her chair, a curious rock formation high up on the saddle of the hill which was known to hunters in past times who sat in or on it. One of the past lairds in the hey-day of the sporting estates used to rest on it when his deer stalking was going badly. I tried to sit on it, but the wind gusts and blasting rain storms made me beat a retreat.

One of the modern stalkers claimed he saw Cailleach na Beinne herself sailing through his car's headlights, but the cynical say it may only have been an old wind-borne jacket. The hill was also believed to be the haunt of faeries.

People telling tales around the shieling fires would often include stories of the Beinn a' Bhric witch and the area has legends of other spectres. She was reputed to have a sacred well in the area which she cleaned out each May.

Together with the witches of Mull and Leanachan (near Spean Bridge), she was alleged to have tried to sink the storm-tossed ships of the Spanish Armada as they sailed down the west coast.

They filled a tub with water and put wooden chips in it. One stirred it, another repeated incantations and a third pushed the chips under the water.

The witch's memory lingers in these hills yet, although scholars differ about her identity. Some argue that, strictly speaking, she is a glastig or spirit, and she is sometimes described as the Autumn Hag. She had grizzled locks, a tawny, tarred plaid and grey hose or stockings. A woman of huge size, she wore a striped or mottled kerchief and deerskin mocassins.

Other sources say she was the spirit of the mountain, a kind of nature goddess and protector of wild places. She dressed in soft russet deer hides and was armed with a spear or quiver, and milked the deer.

Another witch who milked the deer was known as the Cailleach Bheatrach, who lived on top of Morrone, near Braemar, a hill which gives fine views to the main Cairngorms plateau. She may be the same person as the Cailleach Bheur, the Hag of Autumn or Winter, however, as separate anecdotes about her are sparse. The remains of an ancient fort on the top of Morrone were thought to be the remains of her house.

Some hills have good vibes, others have bad ones and nowadays these generally relate to whether the mountaineer had a pleasant time or not on a first visit.

But there was no doubt about Beinn a Ghlo in past times – that big, three-Munro topped mountain mass, north-east of Blair Atholl, and one of Scotland's best-known hills.

The name – given as Beinn y Ghlo in old accounts – generally translates as Mountain of the Veil or Mists and it has several remote corries. It was home to one of the most dreaded witches, and tales about her lingered on into the early days of formal deer stalking.

William Scrope's history of these times, *Days of Deer Stalking*, written in 1883, solemnly sets down a detailed description of her.

She was 'of a very mischievous and malevolent disposition, driving cattle into morasses, where they perish, and riding the forest horses by night, till covered with mire and sweat they drop down from fatigue and exhaustion. She has the power of taking the shape of an eagle, raven, hind or any other animal that may suit her purpose. She destroys bridges and allures people to the margin of the flood by exhibiting a semblance of floating treasures, which they lose their lives in grasping at.'

She was believed to have powers to control the weather and figures largely in shieling tales.

CHAPTER TWENTY

THE HEADLESS HORSEMAN

Sir Walter Scott's epic poem, *The Lady of the Lake,* written in 1810, is set in the Trossachs while Ben Talla (Tallaidh) at 2,498ft, is the third- (some say fourth-) highest mountain on the lovely island of Mull.

The old tale of a spectral horseman was once upon a time known all over the Highlands and Scott felt that he could legitimately include it in a story of love and war set mainly in the Southern Highlands.

Ben Talla derives from the Gaelic word *talaidh* (cattle) which tells of slopes which provided good grazing. This steep-sided cone-shaped mountain dominates Glen Forsa and also part of the old pilgrims' route to Iona across the island via Glen More.

Scottish hills have several specimens of headless spectres and Ben Talla's horseman is one of the most absorbing because some islanders have claimed to have seen him in modern times.

The headless horseman was *Eoghan a'Chinn Bhig* – Ewen of the Little Head – the only son and heir of John, fifth chief of the MacLaines of Loch Buie.

He lived on a small island on Loch Sguabain in Glen More which is reached by a hill pass from the MacLaines' castle at Moy, close to the sea loch of Loch Buie.

Ewen was married to a daughter of MacDougall of Lorne. She had a burning hunger for land, although she already possessed territory in Morvern and on Mull. Her frenzied ambition for more power caused dissent and strain in the clan, and blows between different factions within the MacLaines of Loch Buie and the MacLeans of Duart became certain.

Very sensibly, rather than have heavy casualties in a full-scale civil war among the different branches of the clan, it was decided that groups would fight it out rather in the manner of picked football or shinty teams.

Ewen was on horseback when he met a banshee washing bloodstained clothes in a burn. She gave him a strange warning. If butter was placed on his breakfast table without his asking for it then the day would go well with him. If there was no butter and he asked for it then disaster would befall him.

One would think that in the face of such a dire warning and a looming clash Ewen would have remembered this encounter in every detail, but he forgot or chose to ignore it. Butter was not on his table and he ordered some.

The battle went against Ewen and a Duart clansman's claymore severed his head. The horse bolted with the headless corpse still swaying in the saddle and galloped eastwards along the River Lussa to a spot where the modern Glen More road takes a right-angled bend below Ben Talla and turns sharply southwards.

The horse eventually stopped across the ford above the Falls of Lussa – just below the line of the new road and an empty house called Torness. A tiny cairn marks the spot. Add a stone to it if you find it.

The story has lingered in Highland folk tradition and the headless Ewen and his horse still reputedly gallop along the sides of Ben Talla and around the castle of Moy, where his appearance signals a MacLaine death.

Sir Walter Scott's reference to 'Ben Talla's shingly sides' is not true of most of the mountain. Personally, I found it a steep pull up mainly grassy slopes and much of the lower ground is nowadays under conifer forestry.

One of the highest of the hills that rise from the northern wing of the island of Skye is Ben Edra and just south of it is a bealach (or pass) which was once the haunt of a headless spectre.

It is called *Bealach a' Mhorghain*, the Shingle Pass. The view from Ben Edra is one of the finest of Skye and includes the white sands lying between Morar and Arisaig on the mainland.

It was in an area called the Smooth or Straight Mile, close to the sands, that Mac Gille Chaluim, MacLeod of Raasay, battled with Colann gun Cheann, the evil, headless spectre who used to waylay and kill travellers.

MacLeod of Raasay, a man of strength and courage, met the spectre at midnight and wrestled with him. The spectre's strength began to ebb towards dawn and MacLeod of Raasay was able to pick him up and carry him to the nearest light so he could get a good look at him.

The spectre begged to be released, but MacLeod of Raasay would only agree if he swore by Book and candles (Christian symbols) that he would leave the area for ever.

The spectre agreed to this and flew away, singing sadly to himself. He made his home 70 miles away on Ben Edra and a song and a pipe tune, still played to this day, commemorate his banishment.

The people of old did not attach supernatural qualities to the Brocken Spectre, that natural phenomenon where the sun throws the climber's shadow on to mist and cloud which magnify it. They knew it was the work of nature. The name derives from the highest summit of the Harz Mountains in Germany where weather conditions make it appear more frequently than elsewhere. The Brocken summit was an important place in German folklore and a rendezvous for devils and witches.

CHAPTER TWENTY-ONE

THE FAMILY OF STONE

It is not easy to decide to open up a grave. 'If I was wearing a hat, I would take it off in respect,' said Willie Thom, good hillwalking friend and an advocate, as we eyed a little pile of stones about two feet high and about five feet long. We were standing in a little side glen in Perthshire, behind the great rampart of mountains, the Wall of Rannoch. Before us lay a small mound of stones and boulders, capped with a white quartz stone, sited on a grassy flat beside a burn.

It was a lonely spot, situated far into the hills, rarely visited and off the main routes of Munro-baggers and the nearby great hill-crossing of Glen Meran which links long Glen Lyon with the Water of Tulla.

Our little pile of stones and its glen were special sites to the people of Glen Lyon who fell under Campbell overlordship and also to the earlier MacGregors, who once controlled the glen, but they were ignored by people using the main pass.

From the north came the raiding MacDonalds who cleared out Glen Lyon so successfully that they bankrupted Robert Campbell of Glen Lyon and helped fill him with such hatred for them that he played his part in the infamous Glen Coe massacre of 1692 with immense relish.

One band of MacDonald raiders was taking stolen cattle back up Glen Meran when they found they had also taken a herd maiden along with them, a girl called McNee. She broke the legs of some of the calves to try and slow them down – a practice which seems cruel to us today, but which enabled the pursuing Campbells to catch up.

A running fight took place up the glen and the maiden was killed in the struggle. A little cairn stands beside the burn, near the crest of the Glen Meran pass, to commemorate her, and would be known to the people who built our mound-site. The old and very lovely Breadalbane lullaby, *Crodh*

96

The hill people of long ago believed that trees and plants had good and bad spirits attached to them, and their landscape lived for them in a way almost totally lost to us nowadays. These pine trees in Glen Derry in the Cairngorms symbolised immortality – pines were sometimes planted to mark the graves of heroes. The plant badges of the clans were not for identification, as is often thought, but were talismans

Beautiful Glen Orchy in Argyll is reputed to contain a cave which has a horn hanging on one wall. Whoever finds the horn should blow it and the warriors of the Fianna, the soldier-gods of Gaelic mythology, will leave their graves to come to the aid of Scotland in its hour of need

Beinn Alligin, ranked as the most 'supernatural' of the Torridon mountains, has three rocky peaks known as the Horns of Alligin – a special number to the hill people of long ago

This huge gash on the rocky face of Aonach Dubh in Glen Coe was reputed to have been used by Ossian, the bard son of Fingal, and is called Ossian's Cave. It is an unpleasant, wet place with a sloping floor

Brecan's Cave, at the north end of the island of Jura, Argyll, where the witches of Jura roamed. It was reputedly named after a Norse prince who was drowned in the Gulf of Corrievreckan

Ben Cruachan seen across the waters of Loch Etive in Argyll. Believed to be a sacred mountain, its fastnesses housed a witch and the Fianna, and a nearby gathering site gave Clan Campbell its war slogan 'Cruachan!'

The Five Sisters of Kintail, in the north-west Highlands, which were believed to have been five local maidens who became so depressed in the absence of promised lovers that they were turned into stone and are still waiting

The Brocken Spectre on Liathach, Torridon. The people of old did not attach supernatural powers to this act of nature. They knew the mist magnified figures and that the sun threw the shadow of people on to clouds

Hills with smooth, shaped rock were sometimes regarded as sacred and people imbued the rock with 'feeling'. One such is Creag Bhan, the White Crag, on the island of Gigha off the west side of Kintyre

The Dog Stone, Glen Lyon, where the hounds of Ossian, the bard son of the warrior god, Fingal (Fionn), were reputed to have been tethered. Women going on a journey would lie beneath this stone – it was believed to prevent conception

The name of the devil is attached to many mountains and glens in Scotland. The Devil's Point mountain overlooks Corrour bothy in the Lairig Ghru in the Cairngorms

Abyssinia bothy in Glen Kinglas, Argyll, which is now ruinous but which once had a reputation for being haunted. It is named after a local man who served with the army in Abyssinia (now Ethiopia)

Chailein ('Colin's Cattle'), is said to have been written about her. The cattle belonged to Gray Colin, the Campbell Earl of Breadalbane.

Our little pile of stones is not very impressive at first sight, but tells of an ancient custom.

When the MacGregors of Roro came to the shielings they first of all re-roofed the house of an elderly couple. The shieling houses varied enormously, some large enough to hold entire families, some only big enough for a couple of herd maidens and milking utensils.

The repairing of the old couple's house gradually moved from being a mark of respect to being a good-luck act, a kind of talisman gesture to ensure that the shieling times would be productive in terms of milk, cheese and butter and also in the vibrant social life that went on there – the courting, songs, story-telling and the forerunners of Highland games, the hill races and putting the shot (using a boulder).

When the old couple died, the people continued the practice by building a model or miniature shieling in which they placed two stones to represent the old man, the Bodach (in Gaelic, pronounced po-tach with the 'ch' as in loch), and the Cailleach (the old woman, pronounced Cal-yu*ch*).

These stones were taken from the river where they had been shaped by running water. Then they were carved until they looked like little figures about 18 inches high – looking rather like dumbbells.

Every year, in the spring, the people would take the stone figures out of the miniature shieling and put them outside the building. At the end of summer, when the people went back down again to the main glens and straths, the figures were put back inside the shieling. The roof-stones and turf were put back for the winter and the stone couple stayed inside their house until the next spring.

This ceremony continued well into the nineteenth century when the shieling practice gradually ended on the mainland as a result of changing agricultural and transport patterns. It still lingered on in the Western Isles into living memory.

In modern times this ancient custom has been continued by the local stalker. Any person coming across this miniature shieling should treat it with the greatest reverence because it is truly a memorial to the heart and soul of hill people. If roof-stones are removed to look inside at the stone family they should be replaced exactly as before.

When Willie Thom and our children, Michael Thom and Tom McOwan, first went looking for the miniature shieling following a reference in an old book, we had great difficulty in finding it and were on the verge of abandoning our quest. We were just going to chuck it in when we saw a long stone on top of another which appeared to point up the glen. (This stone has now gone.)

Farther up we saw the sun glint on a piece of quartz and soon found the small, mock-shieling. We discussed whether we should open it up or not and we all had the feeling of being in a church.

On the basis of a very careful removing of stones and laying them on the ground in exactly the same pattern as the roof, we proceeded to look inside. There stood the stone Bodach and Cailleach and their five children. We examined them with care and then put them back and replaced the roof. We were satisfied we had left no trace of our presence.

It was an eerie feeling, one of reverence and almost awe, to look at the shieling and to handle the figures and to reflect on a practice which had gone on for hundreds of years and was still going on.

The title Bodach and Cailleach crop up in a number of hill names. The only other place I've found which has a detailed similarity to the stone family is on the island of Gigha, off the coast of Kintyre, which has a long history of pre-Christian worship. Its little hill of Creag Bhan was reputed to be a place of sacrifice and its smooth, grey rocks gave it a fey feeling.

On nearby farmland stand two little stone figures, the Bodach and the Cailleach, each about two feet high. An island legend says that if they fall over, then bad fortune will befall the island. When we went to look at them one had indeed toppled over and we set it upright.

We were wryly amused – and saddened – in later times to read that the island's mainland owner had got into financial straits. Perhaps he should have ensured the stones were kept upright.

In the early part of this century fishermen from Ireland and the Western Isles would sometimes land on Gigha and make little, votive offerings of money or food to these figures in the hope of ensuring good catches and safety at sea.

Alexander Carmichael, in *Carmina Gadelica*, writes that in the nineteenth century and earlier the last crofter to finish reaping his corn ruefully built a 'woman' with straw, the last corn sheaf, dockens and ragweed stalks, and it was called the *cailleach*. Sometimes a *cailleach* was made and dumped in another person's field. This was considered a deep insult and violence often followed.

That splendid Munro, A 'Mhaighdean (pronounced ah-vatchin), overlooking lonely Carnmore, in the Letterewe estate in Wester Ross, almost certainly has the name, The Maiden, because it looks like one of the end-of-harvest corn stooks.

On one of the buttresses under Sgorr Gaoith (Skor' gooee), meaning peak of wind, is a sharp, rock pinnacle called A' Chailleach, the old woman. It is the highest point on the long hill ridge east of Glen Feshie, on the fringe of the main Cairngorms massif.

She inevitably has her counterpart — a rocky pillar called Am Bodach (the old man) near the top of the spur of Braeriach, opposite.

That staunch patriot, historian, crofter and writer, the late Wendy Wood, wrote that the Bodach is the spirit of the mountain and he quarrelled with the Cailleach.

CHAPTER TWENTY-TWO

THE PIPER IN THE PASS

There are old and persistent legends of a phantom piper and other spectres in the Corrieyairack Pass, the most famous section of General Wade's military roads originally built in the eighteenth century to curb the turbulent Jacobite clans.

This old cattle drovers' route from close to Fort Augustus (formerly Cill Chuimein) in the Great Glen to where Dalwhinnie and the modern A9 road runs, has long been by-passed by modern road patterns and is mainly known nowadays to hill-trampers, Hydro Board workers servicing the line of pylons which runs over the pass, estate and farm vehicles and – alas – four-wheel drive, cross-country, safari-type vehicles.

The crossing was treated with apprehension in past times when it was common for people to die in storms and the tales of ghosts and a phantom piper persisted and spread. Some might have grown in the telling, but here is one told by a practical, experienced soldier, well versed in Highland lore, whose experience had many puzzled witnesses. The incident took place in March 1958 when two years compulsory National Service was still in force.

Lieutenant-Colonel D.J.S. Murray wrote about the controversy in 1983 in a regimental publication of the Queen's Own Highlanders. The event is also commemorated in pipe music. Captain John Maclellan wrote a modern *piobaireachd* (pibroch is the classical music of the pipes) called *The Phantom Piper of the Corrieyairack* based on the experience of soldiers crossing the pass on a route march.

Colonel Murray points out that the incident happened when each regiment (now amalgamated) had their own depots – the Seaforths at Fort George and the Camerons at Inverness – both on the fringe of the finest infantry country in the world.

The Cameron recruits were taken on a series of progressively strenuous outdoor exercises designed to teach them how to cover ground the hard way and if anyone thinks the Marines or any other military body invented 'yomping' then they are many years out. Murray wrote:

> The final exercise always involved a long walk and one of the favourites was over the Corrieyairack, from Fort Augustus in the Great Glen to Garvamore, in Laggan, in Strathspey, 18 miles in all – nine from sea level to 2,500 feet and nine down Wade's famous staircase (or culvert zig-zags) to Garvamore where there is a Wade bridge and where he once had a headquarters base.

In March 1958 he had been judging piping in Aberdeen with the late Colonel Iain Grant of Rothiemurchus, to whom Colonel Murray says he owes a great debt for piping lore and instruction. In conversation he had told Colonel Grant that he would be taking recruits over the Corrieyairack within a few days.

Colonel Grant had remarked that there was a tradition in Badenoch that at dusk in bad weather a column of armed men in Highland dress might be seen moving south over the pass. From descriptions it was believed that this phantom army was, in fact, the men of the Marquis of Montrose's army on their way to victory over the Covenant army of the Marquis of Argyll at Inverlochy, near Fort William, in 1645.

There is a problem with this precise theory.

The army of Montrose and his redoubtable second-in-command, Alasdair Mac Colla, war leader of Clan Donald and son of the incorrigible Colkitto, did *not* go over the whole line of the Corrieyairack. It is more likely that if there is a link between modern phantoms and the spectres of the past that it might be the clansmen of Prince Charles Edward Stuart who certainly used the pass and had some of their first military successes there, capturing the engineer-commander of Ruthven Barracks and other soldiers.

Colonel Murray had expressed polite interest in Colonel Grant's anecdote and before parting Colonel Grant said: 'Well, if anyone sees them, David, you and your chaps will – Highland soldiers on the same road south.'

It was a fine winter's morning as the modern soldiers marched up the hill – crisp and clear, no sun and mist level about a thousand feet. Three regimental pipers played in the early stages.

> We soon reached the mist level, where the sun was trying to break through and I fell behind the column at one stage. The troops were soon out of sight in the cloud; all around was this incredible luminous light and over all, the sound of the pipes.

The soldiers were soon out of the mist in a couple of hours and began the stiff climb up the traverse out of the sheltered hollow which eighteenth-century troops had christened Snugborough and they halted out of the wind.

> Then, as can only happen in the Highlands, all hell was upon us. The wind shrieked, and as we crossed the snowline, it rained frozen particles of snow which stung our bare knees.

Colonel Murray's glasses steamed up and then froze and the troops struggled on holding on to the kilt of the man in front.

One soldier trying to make out the track said he was following two ptarmigan, the mountain grouse, and it was these birds, half-flying or hopping, that led the way over the crest. This caused comment later as the ptarmigan were regarded as 'special' long ago, the mother bird of all others and which could give protection.

Once over the top and down it was merely a matter of pounding out the nine miles to Garvamore Bridge, 'a long, dull slog of the sort all soldiers know'.

> The pipes, of course, were sodden, the pipers were as frozen as the rest of us, and so it was a pretty miserable and bedraggled body of men which finally sighted Garvamore. There, I knew, would be the excellent Company Quartermaster Sergeant Kearney with his devoted band of cooks and helpers but, as the depot in those days had no radio, it had of course been impossible to let the CQMS know we were coming, and so I resigned myself to a long wait until the meal was finally brewed up.
>
> But not a bit of it! Judge my astonishment, as they say, when we fell

out to find all ready – stew steaming, tea boiling. I knew that the CQMS was first rate in the field, but this was high-class administration by any standards.

And so, all innocent, I asked him how he had known we were coming. 'Too easy,' said he, 'We heard the pipes as you came down the glen.'

'Surely not?' I encountered, 'The pipes haven't played a note for five hours.'

'Didn't we hear the pipes, boys?'

'Yes, for about 20 minutes coming down the glen before you came in sight, Sir!'

'That's right,' said the CQMS, 'and I'm a piper myself, Sir, mind, I heard the pipes! So did the boys, all of us.'

Well, then it hit me! Rothiemurchus's 'Highland soldiers on the same road'. And being the son of a fey Highland mother, I looked at the mist-covered mountains, and heard the howl of the rising wind, and felt the hair crawl on the back of my neck, and didn't hesitate.

I had only ever given my next order once before to Camerons, during what might best be described as 'a spontanous readjustment of the tactical situation' at Kohima [a bitterly fought clash with the Japanese in Burma during the Second World War]. 'Let's get the hell out of here!'

And so that's the story of the phantom piper of the Corrieyairack, and I've listened to some rubbish, as earnest people have tried to explain it all away: the wind in the telegraph wires, but there are no telegraph wires: someone practising in the house, but nobody lived there. It was all a put-up job by the cooks.

I've seen frightened men, and there were several at Garvamore in the winter dusk, and I was one of them. And just what, or who, were the two ptarmigan that led us over the Pass?

The mystery remains.

CHAPTER TWENTY-THREE

ROCKS OF AGES

Mountaineers on extended holidays often have rest days when a cave or historic site is visited and such expeditions have a way of turning out to be more energetic outings than if the group had gone on the hill in the first place.

Some years ago a group of my friends were on Mull and we decided to visit MacKinnon's Cave, set close to the spectacular Gribun cliffs, on the north side of the Burg peninsula – a spectacular corner of that lovely island.

The cave, like several others in the Highlands, has a spectral bagpiper. This long cavern is easily found from a small track close to Balmeanach farm, but the going along the tide-washed and stony beach can be awkward for some people. It is reputed to take its name from Abbot MacKinnon, of Iona, who used it as a place of retreat and meditation.

There is a large, flat stone in a vast chamber section which the people called Fionn's table, a reference to the warrior-god of Gaelic mythology. The cave takes a couple of twists and shuts out all light and the back section dwindles into a long mine-like shaft which some visitors find very claustrophobic. Boswell and Johnson were shown the cave and were impressed by its size when they visited Mull.

Our ancestors wanted to find out how long the cave was so they sent a piper and some friends inside while they gathered on the surface. The idea was that the sound of the pipes would filter up through cracks and fissures in the ground and when the music stopped they would mark the upper ground as being the limit of the cave's size.

The piper set off into the cave accompanied by wary friends who carried flaring torches. Unknown to them, the cave was the home of a spectral banshee and she was irritated at being disturbed and attacked them.

She began to kill them one by one, but held back from the piper while he continued to play. He eventually became breathless and both he and his pipes expired just as he neared the mouth of the cave. A local tradition says the party were accompanied by a dog and it got out, but left most of its hair in the hands of the banshee.

On our day trip we went right to the back of the main cave and, to save the batteries of our head torches, we agreed that we would switch them all off except one.

In one of those daft moments that happen on such occasions we all accidentally switched off our torches at the same time and for a few seconds there was total darkness, broken only by chuckles. Then came a loud and high-pitched scream which raised the hair on the back of our necks.

When we switched the torches on again we found that one of our group had stood on Harvey, a Jack Russell terrier which had accompanied us into the cave and which had been padding along silently in our wake.

Caves played a prominent part in the mythology of Celtic hill people as places of natural and religious significance because they provided entrances to the Otherworld and a group of tales were once classified as 'Caves' but most have not survived.

There was immense reverence for stone. This feeling, too, can be felt among some modern hillwalkers – that a slab or buttress is not just a challenge to be physically climbed but that the stone has a texture and feel, almost a kind of life and character of its own. It is no accident that many people have collections of striking stones at home, picked up on the hills over the years.

The ancient peoples had a fervent on-going communication or communion with nature and believed in the consciousness of all things. Everything was a fragment of a cosmic whole.

Stones were old beyond time and had indwelling spirits, they believed. It was widely accepted that the Lia Fail, the famous Stone of Destiny, on which Scottish kings were traditionally crowned, could roar with joy when it felt the touch of a righteous ruler's foot. Another stone could tell if a man lied.

The outlook of the people of old was not scientific. They explained geological facts in the language of folklore and it is a deep and charming subject.

No one can be in the Assynt area of Sutherland, without being conscious of areas having a moon-like landscape appearance, of bleak moors and rocky peaks sticking up like the remaining teeth in a half-buried skull, or boulder fields, large slabs, unexpected caves and burns which dive underground and then re-emerge.

Sutherland was, of course, the south land of the raiding Norsemen and Assynt may well take its name from a Norse word for rocky, although a Gaelic compound has also been suggested which means ground of a broken nature.

An old legend says that two brothers fought for mastery of the area and the winner, called Unt, is commemorated in the name. Another legend says the Norse gods came here when the world was young and practised mountain building. They returned to Lochlann (the old name for Scandinavia) and shaped the mountains there, this time with more practised hands.

Sometimes people with ear-ache went to selected caves and let drops of water fall from the roof into their ear. The coldness might well have brought relief to swellings. Moreover, some moulds found growing in caves have a penicillin base or material similar to streptomycin and 'cave soil' was used to treat wounds and ulcers.

Some caves were malevolent. The mountaineer and writer Brenda Macrow, who spent many happy years staying in Torridon, Wester Ross, tells of a 'Golden Cave' at the foot of the striking mountain, Liathach, into which two men disappeared and never returned.

The neighbouring mountain, Beinn Alligin, has a great gash just below the summit of Sgurr Mór, and is named in Gaelic as Eag Dhubh na h-Eigheachd, the Black Notch of the Outcry. Older people in the glen said that shepherds sometimes heard a man's voice shouting there until one day a man fell to his death. After that, the voice was heard no more.

There are cairns in the hills which mark deer hunts or heroes, or significant acts, such as the flat stone on the south side of the Lairig Eilde (Pass of the Hinds) which links Glen Coe with Glen Etive, and marked the signing of a land agreement between the MacIans or MacDonalds of Glen Coe and the Campbells of Inverawe. Of similar reverence was a prominent boulder not far from the memorial at Dalmally, Argyll, to the Gaelic poet Duncan Ban MacIntyre, where the travelling people, the tinkers, gathered to have their babies baptised.

At Dalchiorlich farm, at the head of Glen Lyon, stands a stone of about three feet high and shaped like the neck and head of a dog. It is called the Dog Stone and the hunting hounds of the partly mythical people of the past were reputed to have been tethered to it.

It was believed to have special properties and women and girls going on a long journey would lie underneath it in the belief that it would give them protection from conception.

On the old hill pass between Glen Shira and Inveraray, in Argyll, and the market centre of Dalmally, the Bealach Cabrach (Pass of the Antlers), there stands on the north side a curiously shaped, forked set of stones. The original Gaelic name has gone adrift, but the people of the townships nearby, now gone, called them the Angel Horns.

The people believed that if you passed between these stones you would have protection against evil when on a journey. The gap measures between a few inches at the bottom to about a couple of feet at the top.

The shape of these stones has a phallic significance. Mothers used to take their daughters there and ask them to swear that they had been sexually pure. The reason may not be solely linked to sexual morals, but the inheritance of goods or land. Like the Dog Stone in Glen Lyon, the Angel Horns in the Bealach Cabrach were also used as a means to prevent conception after women had passed through them.

Rocks, too, were the last resting place for unbaptised children who were taken there between sunset and sunrise on a dark night with no moon. It was thought such children had a spirit but no soul, and this spirit, or taran, entered into a rock and lived there. They became mac-talla, son of rock, which is the Gaelic term for an echo.

The medicinal power of many rocks was very strong. Sir Walter Scott's piper, John Bruce, from Skye, spent a Sunday collecting 12 stones from 12 south-running burns for Sir Walter to sleep upon and be relieved from the pain of gallstones.

Cairns, too, were regarded with feeling and dignified manners long ago. The modern habit of building waymarker cairns is pernicious and it is good to see revulsion against this habit and that many hill trampers now knock such cairns down. There is a case for a cairn at the crest of a bealach (pass) or to mark an awkward turn down a gully amid cliffs or bluffs, but not much more than that.

A cairn really *meant* something long ago – a rallying point, the death of a hero, a resting place for coffins on funeral routes, a key point in a staghunt.

Climbers on Ben Resipol, in Ardnamurchan, can see the *Uaimh Dhàil,* the Big Cairn of the Meeting, a great cairn which marked the meeting place of the people of Moidart and Loch Shiel and those from Sunart when bodies were taken to the burial islands of Eilean Fhianain on Loch Shiel. Such a rendezvous was treated with the greatest dignity and it was widely believed that the voices of the dead could be heard in such places.

Building cairns as a kind of roll-call when clans went to war was also very common. As with the funeral cairns, the voices of the dead were believed to be heard there.

There is controversy over cairns on some other hills, including single stones, of which the best known are a group of man-made cairns on Geal Charn, above the Drumochter Pass on the busy A9. From the road they look like people and are often pointed out as such. Some have been demolished in recent times because people bumping them in mist think they are on the summit, but they have been rebuilt. They may be gathering points for shooting parties.

In the same way as cairns have lost their supernatural qualities for modern people, the character of wells has gone the same way. Once a focal point in many areas they have been drained, become overgrown or vanished from the map. Bones of Celtic saints, for example, were sometimes washed in wells, acts of great religious significance.

The prominent knoll of Dundurn, which overlooks the golf course at St Fillans on Loch Earn, the site of an old hill fort and also associated with St Fillan, has a holy well below it. The old *Statistical Account* tells of 70 people visiting it in 1791. On the rocky summit is a natural chair where pilgrims suffering from rheumatism of the back sat down and were then pulled down the hill.

Munro-baggers who have climbed Carn an t-Sagairt Mór, the Big Hill of the Priest or Clerk, close to the old hill crossing of the Tolmount from Loch Callater and Braemar over to Glen Clova and Glen Doll in Angus, may take its name from a cleric, Pàdruig, who led the local people to Loch Callater to pray for an end to a severe frost. All other wells in the district were frozen solid, but the Priest's Well, *Fuaran an t-Sagairt*, which can be seen just to the east of the lodge, flowed freely once again. There is a hill in Glen Callater called Craig Phàdruig.

CHAPTER TWENTY-FOUR

HEARING, SEEING, FEELING

It was hillman and master mariner Captain Ronnie Leask, of Edinburgh, who correctly summed up the feelings of many people. 'There are too many folk of integrity who have had odd experiences in the hills for every one of them to be written off as fools and to be ridiculed. There are still unexplained happenings experienced by people of the utmost veracity and vast experience.'

In examining and collating these anecdotes of ghosts, spectres, poltergeists and psychic phenomena over many years, I find a number of common factors arise.

A feeling of being accompanied by some unknown or additional person – particularly when alone – is a not uncommon feeling on the hills among mountaineers. Explorers, too, have felt this and it would appear to have little to do with whether any specific event took place on that site in past times.

It is generally a benevolent feeling, of a benign and unseen companion, and it sometimes happens when a mountaineer or walker is tired. It may just be a trick of the mind, even a kind of wishful thinking, and it occurs in bursts.

A second factor which crops up not so frequently, is that walkers feel very cold before experiencing or seeing some kind of phantom figure, or when they find a hollow in the hills or a pile of rocks which seems 'hostile' to them. The behaviour of dogs also affects people; dogs showing fear, facing the one way, hair on end, refusing to go on – although there can be a natural explanation for that.

A third is that most people who have a tale to tell preface it by showing great reluctance in telling it. They don't want to be the butt of jokes, to be laughed at, scorned or ridiculed.

A fourth element is the natural explanation, the sound of the wind in the rocks, mist magnifying size, noises from deer or other wildlife or simply mistaking some object.

The late W. Kersley Holmes, of Dollar, mountaineer, writer and poet, told of being on Ben Donich, near Arrochar, on a very hot day. He could see a picnic group down below in Glen Croe and could distinctly make out the red and white of women's dresses.

He hurried down, hoping to cadge a cup of tea and perhaps to chat up the girls, only to find that the 'picnic party' was a group of painted barrels which had been dumped by a road-making gang.

Conversely, those who report odd experiences are generally experienced in the sights and sounds of the hills, moors, glens and straths. Most are very independently minded people – a common trait in outdoor clubs as various chairpersons and committees have discovered to their cost. They are not easily kidded or influenced. Yet many report experiencing some corner of a hill or glen which had 'hostile' vibes. This comes up again and again, and from people who have never experienced it in urban situations.

Ronnie Leask admits to feeling 'uncomfortable' at the ruin of Slugain Lodge on the track over to Beinn a' Bhùird, in the Cairngorms, and also at Papadil Lodge, on the island of Rum, when it was intact and furnished.

I once felt very uncomfortable walking along the road through the woods east of Derry Lodge (at the east end of the Lairig Ghru) which at that time was full of mature trees. I didn't remark on this to my friend but when we stopped at the burn half a mile on he mentioned he'd found it weird and unpleasant walking through this section and I then confessed likewise.

As I recall, it was brilliant sunshine at the time and – always looking for a natural explanation – I think it may have been due to some optical effect of the dark track through the trees and the sun shining through the woods which were then heavily mossed on the north side. I haven't experienced this there since, nor previously.

Syd Scroggie tells in his foreword to Affleck Gray's book, *The Big Grey Man of Ben MacDhui*, that he had sensed an 'atmosphere', sometimes malignant, sometimes benign, in places as different as Torlinn, a Neolithic chambered cairn in Arran, and an old farmhouse on the middle reaches of the Spey called Westerton.

Syd wrote:

> A ruined cottage on the upper Uisge Labhair, just where this burn emerges from the Bealach Dubh, is invested with a happy feeling, according to a friend of mine, Alan Logan. Whereas a certain silent hollow on the Rannoch Moor, a place of gnarled, mossy alders and stagnant water, struck my wife, Margaret – not usually sensitive to this kind of thing – as eerie to the point of frightening.

Mountaineer Iain M. Gilbert, of Beech Grove, Wishaw, told me of a similar feeling on Saturday, 29 August 1981, 'a brilliant day' in the Glenfinnan area in the Western Highlands. He says:

> It was hot, cloudless, no wind. I had some time between trains and decided to try and reach Sgurr an Utha, the Corbett* just to the north of the station.
>
> As I approached the slightly lower eastern top, Fraoch Bheinn, which has a somewhat undulating summit plateau, it was becoming clear that I would be hard pressed to reach the Corbett in the available time. So I decided instead to linger for a short while on the minor top, even although conditions were too hazy to appreciate the distant views.
>
> At this point I was suddenly aware of an eerie silence – an absolute stillness – no movement of any kind, birds, animals, insects, no distant aircraft, not even the slightest breath of wind. I was then overcome with a distinct feeling of unease and a desire to leave the summit as quick as possible.
>
> I have a recollection of looking over my shoulder as I strode off with a slightly quickened pace, although, quite what I was expecting to see, I don't know. Normal feelings returned within about half a mile or so.

*A mountain which is over 2,500ft and under 3,000ft

I do a lot of my walking alone and have visited most of the Munros. I have never experienced anything like it before or since. However, I am sure my reaction was entirely psychological, almost certainly due to the prevailing circumstances, i.e. the sound of silence, and not to anything supernatural.

Although I can offer a rational explanation for my own incident, I find the whole subject quite fascinating.

Others, too, have had similar experiences. Jim Mitchell, of Kenningnowes Road, Stirling, who has had 20 years of experience on the hills, is puzzled by an incident when he was in Knoydart, in the western Highlands.

I am researching a history of that estate and in 1980 I walked alone from Barrisdale to Inverie, sticking rigidly to the coast – quite an arduous route.

I was looking for and checking old steadings marked on the 6″–1 mile OS map, photographing and sketching layouts on the way. It was a beautiful, clear day in May – just enough warmth to make walking pleasant.

I had reached the scattered, deserted township of Ridarnoch, one of the largest on the coast, and was photographing the most substantial of the ruins which was still standing up to the lintels. The house post-dated the great clearance of 1853.

I sat down with my back to the wall facing out to Rum and the other islands with the late afternoon sun in my face, and finished off my piece.

Suddenly, I felt very cold. It was as if a lump of supercooled air had descended on me. There was no wind or air movement. I got up and zipped up my jacket – slightly perplexed by this strange phenomena.

I moved into the ruin and looked about. The stones still felt warm from the sun which was still out, but the air was literally freezing. Also, a very strong feeling of foreboding – an awareness of malevolence – fear, call it what you like, got a grip of me.

I left the building, picked up my rucksack and climbed away out of the strath. The coldness vanished outwith 50 feet of the house, as did the driving urge on me to leave. However, my own motivation to keep going had taken over and being an abject coward, I did not experiment by going back!

I have since been back to the ruin on a less pleasant day – again alone (to lay the ghost, I suppose!) and felt nothing. I should add that the excitement of seeing on the ground the evidence of research more than outweighed any melancholia I might have felt about the deserted townships and I am sure that it was not 'imagination working overtime'.

Kersley Holmes also tells of two experiences when bad vibes were felt. In his much-loved book, *On Scottish Hills*, first published in 1946 and reissued in 1962, he describes being on Creag Mhór, between Glen Lyon and Glen Lochay in Perthshire, on a warm and sunny afternoon.

What befell was odder in its effect on me than can be explained by a mere description of the incident. I can best indicate what I was conscious of by saying that as I plodded happily and lazily up the open brae it was as if something or somebody had suddenly stamped hard twice on the short dry turf at my back. Its effect was to make me clammy under my shirt.

Mr Holmes went on to say that he saw no sheep around, and he wondered if a boulder in an underground cavity had fallen over.

'I thought of such explanations, and went on, but the atmosphere of the afternoon had lost something of its cheerfulness.'

When he told his experience to a friend – 'a level-headed athletic type' – the friend told him that he had set out to fish one of the hill burns that led to the River Lyon. His morning brightness was dulled by an indefinable unease of mind.

Then things began to go wrong, little things, but in the aggregate more than merely annoying, and presently he came to a kind of hollow with white stones in it where he felt so strongly that he was not wanted that he immediately turned and went down, giving up his fishing for the day.

An apparently inexplicable feeling of dread also affected Mr G.V.R. Grant, of Kirkbean, Dumfries, who wrote to me saying he and his wife had a frightening experience in June 1946 when he was 29 and his wife 26.

They had hired bikes to go by themselves to climb Lochnagar and also to reach the far end of Loch Muick.

It was a hot, sunny day when we made the expedition to Loch Muick. As we had plenty of time to spare, we decided after a picnic luncheon and having looked at the map to climb up to Loch Dubh.

When we got to it we were very hot. Looking at the far end, we could see a sandy beach so we thought it would be a good thing to walk along the side until we got there and then cool off and freshen up with a bathe . . . We were up to about our knees in the water when suddenly we both must have felt an overwhelming sense of menace, terror and evil for without speaking or looking at each other and without even a split second's hesitation we both turned round and scampered as fast as we could back to the beach. We were so frightened that we never spoke a word to the other.

Instead of letting the sun dry us slowly and gently as we lay on the sand, which was our original intention, we dabbed ouselves dry as quickly as we could with our handkerchiefs and then, half wet, dressed, still in silence, and walked back along the Dubh Loch as fast as possible glancing every so often, still terror-stricken at the water.

I have no explanation, but that experience is still vivid in my mind and recollection. All I can suggest is that as certain churches contain within them a great sense of worship, peace and love, so maybe other places contain the opposite and the Dubh Loch is one of them.

I was visiting a primary school in Fife, under the auspices of the Scottish Arts Council's 'Writers In Schools' Scheme, when I met a fellow-hillwalker in Mrs Moira J. Hughes, of West Harbour, Charlestown, in Fife. She told me of an experience she and her husband, John, had on Craighorn, near Alva, in the Ochils. I publicised this incident in the *Friends of the Ochils* newsletter, but received no other information or comment.

Mrs Hughes said it occurred on a Sunday in July or August, 1991, and around 2 p.m. in sunny, calm weather with a clear sky. She said:

We had just reached the cairn and I (as always) had patted the cairn when the ground around us for a radius of about 20 ft began to vibrate and thrum for no apparent reason.

This thrumming continued for about two minutes. We then sat down and had our picnic!

There may be a natural explanation in that the front of the Ochils is formed by a geological fault and tremors are known, sometimes to the extent of mildly rattling crockery in houses in the Hillfoots villages, but there are no tremors recorded for July or August in 1991. No other person has reported this experience at that time.

Some experiences involve more than one, individual noise. Mr Alistair Farquhar, of Clifton Road, Aberdeen, told me:

In June 1977 I was camped beside an old ruined shooting lodge . . . west of Braemar.

My intention was to set off early the following morning and climb Beinn Iutharn Mhór but, on awakening at 07.00 hours, found the summits of the hills mist-enshrouded. I made myself a cup of tea and settled back in my sleeping bag to read a book, hoping that the mist would clear.

At about 08.30 hours I heard the sound of *marching* feet coming up the track which ran close to my tent.

Rather than appear inquisitive, I waited until they passed behind the lodge before emerging to see where the walkers had gone.

I skirted the lodge and although the track stretched in front of me for at least a quarter of a mile with good visibility all around, much to my surprise I could see no one, although the tramping of feet gradually receding was still audible in front of me.

When I first heard the noise of the boots I thought it was a small group of hillwalkers (perhaps eight to ten of them) until I realised they were all in step.

To this day I have no logical explanation for this.

Two friends of mine, Fred and Monica Gordon, had a strange experience in Glen Fearder, on Deeside, in the summer of 1979.

Fred is now chief ranger for Gordon district council, a highly experienced mountaineer, a naturalist and holder of an award for mountain rescue. Monica is now head teacher of Clatt primary school, near New

Leslie, in Grampian. Both are very level-headed people and we have enjoyed days on the hill together. Fred told me:

> We were camped near the ruined farm of Ratlich when, during the night, Monica woke to the sound of a number of voices down near the Fearder Burn. When I woke up a bit later I also heard them. It sounded like a group of people of all ages generally chatting. It has to be said that there was also the sound of the burn, but these 'voices' were quite distinct from it although it obviously muffled them to an extent.
>
> It is a puzzle to us. We have since discovered that we were camped close to the ruins of an old chapel dedicated to a shadowy Celtic saint, St Manire. There was also a market held here at one time although it was moved to Clachanturn, near Crathie.

Both Fred and Monica are adamant about what they heard and that it was not imagined.

Mystery voices, too, were heard by Mr E.G. Hall, of Church Stile Studios, Grasmere, in Cumbria, who wrote to the *Scots Magazine* about an incident on the west peak of Ben Damph above Loch Torridon on a wintry day.

> I lay down to watch, alternately, the sun setting behind the Storr on Skye, and the full moon rising beyond the Fannichs. As I lay there on that March evening, I heard the voices of two people – one a young female voice, and it seemed a happy conversation.
>
> It lasted a few minutes. I could hardly believe anyone else was up there so late; Ben Damph had been deserted anyway, and I scarcely expected to see people around at that time of year during the week.
>
> I got up and found no one. With snow about, there was no trace of footprints and only one way off.
>
> Several months later I was told of an old legend of a local man leaving his unfaithful wife up there as a punishment . . .

A possible explanation for some 'sightings' is that people may have temporarily experienced some kind of telepathy. They may have been interested in the subject, as was that great naturalist, writer and historian,

Seton Gordon, or they may know nothing about it and care less, but nevertheless been put in a setting and atmosphere where that happened, however fleetingly.

Seton Gordon once wrote of an old friend:

> As the years pass, some of us think back often to old days, and live again happy experiences with friends who have left us. One of my closest friends, Dick Crew, had a great love of the hills and many was the walk and climb we made.
>
> Wandering across those lonely and lovely places, a spiritual link was forged between us.
>
> I recall one winter's day a year or two after the passing of my friend when alone I crossed the hill pass we had so often traversed together, and when, throughout that mist-filled walk, I had the sense of his near presence: many people who have walked and lived much alone have had the same experience.
>
> Telepathy between the living is more common than many of us realise, but when one of the friends has crossed to another plane the experience is rarer.

When on a visit to Spitsbergen in 1993 I came across a comment on telepathy written by Seton Gordon.

> Often in the past when amid the snow-clad peaks and glacier-filled valleys of Spitsbergen, I was in communication with my wife, who was fifteen hundred miles and more distant from me. This interchange of thoughts – telepathy, call it what you will – gives a feeling of power, a feeling of humbleness, a feeling of faith, and one recalls that saying of St Paul, 'The things that are unseen are eternal.'

Fraser Darling, when he was carrying out his researches on North Rona, that lonely island to the north-east of the Butt of Lewis, found himself after lengthy periods of isolation able to mentally foresee future events in his life. Martin Martin, factor to the MacLeods and travel writer, who died in 1719, wrote that the families on North Rona had second sight and experienced apparitions of visitors before these people reached the island.

There is one common factor to most of these events. Near silence, quiet, and peace in an outdoor setting are needed before the mind can go along such paths.

One man who had a sighting, and who used to take part in informal extra-sensory perception experiments was the late Jock Nimlin, field officer with the National Trust for Scotland and pioneer of many a rock climb, particularly on the Cobbler.

Jock was descending to Corrour bothy with a friend, Bill Corr, when he saw a cottage-type tent with a light inside pitched beside the bothy. He said to Bill, 'Look at that!' Bill commented that it was odd to pitch a tent beside the bothy (when there was room to spread oneself inside). When they neared the bothy both the tent and its mysterious inhabitant had vanished.

Jock was a total sceptic about 'unusual sightings and experiences' and told me the moon was full, it was October, they were nearly at 2,000ft, the sky was open and there was a ground mist which produced a thick hoar frost. He theorised that the moon was shining either on a rock or a small bank of mist creating the illusion of a tent.

On the point that his companion also saw a tent (although Jock had not specified what he had seen), Jock says that he and Bill Corr had a kind of mental rapport. They used to put on ESP demonstrations for fun. Jock would concentrate on shapes and Bill would draw them on paper. Bill normally got the basic shape if not the detail. For example, if Jock thought of the Matterhorn, Bill would draw a bell tent or thin triangle.

They could also sometimes transmit the shapes and numbers of playing cards which must have provided many a merry moment. Jock believes that his rapport with Bill explains them both, independently, seeing the same 'tent' object.

Some apparitions are, of course, capable of a natural explanation, but others are baffling.

Syd Scroggie tells of a wartime experience when he planned to spend the night in the Shelter Stone, near Loch Avon, in the Cairngorms. He recalls:

The light was beginning to go and I was sitting outside the Stone look-ing down towards the loch when out of the twilight on one side of the loch, moving towards the twilight on the other and silhouetted against the silvery waters of the loch, was a man walking.

He hadn't got a rucksack on. He was large and I thought, 'Great, I'm going to get company' because where would he be going at that time of night except the Shelter Stone? I ran away down in what light was left. Down through the tracks and boulders I went and I called out and I went left and right and looked into the shingle at the shore of the loch.

There was no reply. The hair began to bristle on the back of my neck and I got away back to the Shelter Stone and jammed the entrance with my rucksack and I was glad the sun came in the morning.

Mr Willie Williamson, of Oxton, Birkenhead, near Liverpool, was persuaded to tell his story by his brother-in-law.

I would like to say that I was born in Glasgow and discovered the Scottish hills as a teenager and apart from some years in the Merchant Navy as a radio officer, these hills have lured me back for years. In other words, I consider myself an experienced hillwalker in all weathers and not likely to be panicked – least of all in good weather.

In July 1982 I spent a week camping at Kinlochleven spending the days Munro-bagging in the Mamores. The weather was unusually hot all week and I had a splendid time in the hills.

On the Friday I decided to climb Binnein Beag at the eastern end of the Mamore range. I walked from the campsite to the hill via Coire an Lochain to the west of Sgurr Eilde Mór, then headed for the bealach between Binnein Beag and Binnein Mór. It was a bright sunny day, very little cloud and I left my rucksack at the small lochan by the bealach, then did my hill before returning to the bealach.

I was quite alone as I sat by the lochan, eating sandwiches in the warm sunshine. Suddenly, I knew that someone was watching me; a strong feeling that it was a wild-looking Highlander staring intently at me and that he was starving and needed food.

A feeling of intense cold was all too obvious to me despite the sunny day. Naturally, I looked round, seeing (and expecting to see) nothing unusual. However, the feeling persisted that the starving man was lying on the hillside watching my every movement. I was so uncomfortable that I left the lochan, but *did* leave a sandwich there.

That walk back in its early stages from the road unsettled me. I could feel the hair on the nape of my neck was erect. I looked back several times and, of course, could see nobody. When I told this story to my friend a few hours later (he had driven up from Glasgow) he told me I went very white.

As a regular hillwalker I know that being in the right mental frame of mind is as important as physical fitness. Also, I can say that nothing like this has been experienced before or since.

I have not been back to that particular area and I would only return if I was with other people. I am adamant I would not go there on my own.

A feeling of being puzzled, of 'why me?' affects some hill gangrels who have seen a possible apparition. One such is Bruce Hardy, of Millbreck, Mintlaw, Aberdeenshire. Here is his story:

On Saturday, 5 May 1990, I set out to walk from Loch Muick over Lochnagar, past the Stuic and round the southern side of Carn an t-Sagairt Mór down to Loch Callater Lodge and on to Braemar.

It was a belting hot, still day and with nearly 50 pounds of rope, assorted ironmongery and food I was wilting by the time I reached the top of Lochnagar. Having left my waterbottle at home, I was aware of the fact that I was suffering seriously from dehydration and possibly mild heatstroke, but I reckoned I was in control.

Having left the last tourist on top of Lochnagar, I dropped down from the Stuic towards the Allt an Dubh Loch burn for a much-needed drink. I drank my fill and set off once again along the path. Looking up, I saw a man moving fast down the hill in a north-westerly direction on a course that would intersect with mine some hundred yards beyond the burn.

The man had tousled black hair of average length, a black beard and was wearing a combat-style camouflage smock and what appeared to be shorts. He was not wearing a rucksack but did look to be holding something in one hand (a dixie perhaps?).

My first reaction was 'Oh blast it, I'm about to get mugged!' which would seem somewhat unusual in as much as I have been going to the hills since I was four years old and have never before felt threatened by a stranger.

I continued to walk for about 100 yards or so before glancing round, expecting the stranger to be on the path behind me. I had my second upset of the day. He had vanished. From where I stood on the side of the hill I could see clearly in every direction for more than half a mile. Nothing moved.

I sat down and watched for some minutes. Nothing! I tried some simple arithmetic to see if I really was delirious. My brain functioned okay. It was now, if anything, even more still than before, flat, calm and silent.

So where did he go? More to the point, where did he come from? Pieces of twisted aluminium litter the side of Carn an t-Sagairt Mór — the remains of a crashed aircraft.

Unpleasant thoughts about ghosts entered my mind so I got up and cleared off.

I looked for him on several occasions as I climbed up the path, but there was no sign. He had completely vanished.

Hillwalker Mike Thorpe, from West Bridgeford, in Nottingham, states he felt a ghostly hand on his shoulder when in the Mamores in August 1986. He told me:

The incident took place on a solo walk up along the Mamores. In order to get up on to the ridge itself, I followed the path along the east bank of the Allt Coire a' Mhusgain, separating the slopes of Sgurr a' Mhaim and Stob Bàn. I quote now from my diary of that time, written shortly after the trip.

'As I plodded on, along the lower stretches of the path, I began to think of all the well-known British mountaineers who'd died in their prime and thought of which well-known ones were left. These thoughts lasted quite a while . . .

'I had the entire path to myself as I climbed higher and higher away from the roar of the white water. In spite of all the burns in spate, everything became very quiet and still. So quiet and still that I felt someone was behind me.

'In fact, I turned around twice to see if there was another party following me! No one there! A little later on a left-hand bend I stopped to take a photo of some waterfalls and cascades.

'I was certain that someone placed their hand on my right shoulder. I turned again, to say "hello", but again nobody was there. I started to worry a little now and hurriedly packed away, moving on and upwards to the col between Stob Ban and Sgurr an Iubhair.

'I was not followed again throughout the rest of this walk.'

Equally puzzled by a similar experience is Garrow MacLaren, of Kildonan Drive, Helensburgh, but his took place in Glen Affric on August 6, 1984. He says:

I had left my car at Loch Beinn a' Mheadhoin to climb Toll Creagach and Tom a' Choinich on the northern side of Glen Affric. It was a beautiful autumnal day with clear and delightful views up Gleann nam Fiadh and the stalkers' path to the Bealach Toll Easa.

After climbing up the rocky ridge to Tom a' Choinich, I returned to the bealach and ascended fairly steeply, but easily, to the summit of Toll Creagach.

The steep return down to the Gleann nam Fiadh track was accomplished very quickly over heathery slopes where it was essential to cool down by plunging my head into the burn.

Eventually, when I raised my head and looked up the track some 25 yards away, I saw a lone figure striding in my direction.

I recollect that he was dressed for walking, possibly all in grey, with what looked like a pack on his back. With the prospect now of having company on the longish trek to my car, I turned to collect my pack. However, when I stood up and looked to the track a few yards away, expecting to see him, there was no sign whatsoever of the walker in any direction.

I can say that there was no possibility of him passing me in that short period or indeed being able to conceal himself as there was a clear view in all directions within a reasonable distance.

Being rather puzzled by now, after having another careful look all around I set off down the track thinking he may have passed by and that I could yet catch him up.

There may be some logical explanation for the walker's disappearance on the Glean nam Fiadh track, but I cannot really think of one.

A similar experience in a nearby area happened to Robert Smith, of Hucclecote, Gloucester, a maintenance joiner with Gloucestershire local authority. He was then aged 54, the date was 12 May 1989, and the time between 4.30 p.m. and 5.30 p.m. He told me:

I had a strange experience whilst walking the 'Ultimate Challenge' (a cross-country route project) in 1989.

My walk from Dornie (in Kintail) took me through Lagg and Bundalloch, then followed the river Glennan to Camas-luinie.

Roughly half a mile east of Camas-luinie on the south side of the river Elchaig the track undulates. As I dropped into the dip, I was aware that about 70 to 80 yards ahead, and coming towards me, were two girls aged about 11 and 13.

I expected to meet them as I came on to the rise so you can imagine my surprise when as I did so there was nobody to be seen.

The track ahead was out of my sight for only about a minute. At first I stood there in disbelief, then walked slowly forward thinking they might have been frightened by my presence in such a remote area.

There was nowhere anybody could have hidden except some large rocks. I called 'hallo' and eventually looked around by the rocks, which would not have effectively hidden anyone anyway because of their shape.

Eventually, I continued my walk but constantly looked back, convinced they would somehow reappear, but they never did.

A mountain man who 'saw' his wife in the hills was artist R.J. Singleton, who lives at Arrina, Shieldaig, Strathcarron, in Ross-shire. He says:

I consider myself to be a relatively fit and agile climber and have been climbing Scottish mountains and hills regularly for the past 30 years. I spent as much time as possible climbing in the hills and, also being an artist, searching for reference material for my mountain art work and paintings. My story is strange rather than supernatural. It is the only peculiar experience I have to offer having spent many memorable days in the hills.

The day was drawing to a close as far as walking was concerned. I'd been up on An Teallach (the spectacular mountain overlooking little Loch Broom) for most of the day doing the usual round from Dundonell (hotel and cottages) over the main tops, including Sgurr Fiona, and was now walking down the well-used track from Shenavall (a bothy behind An Teallach).

It was early evening, but being early in May it was still bright, the day having improved from dull and wet with snow showers on the ridge.

I was less than an hour of easy walking distance from the road (where my wife who had decided to spend the day in Ullapool was due to meet me) when, to my delight, I caught sight of her walking up the track. She waved as if to greet me.

However, no sooner had I spotted her and waved back than the next minute she had disappeared. I carried on walking, expecting at any minute to see her reappear much closer. Indeed, there was no sign and I began to be both baffled and annoyed ('playing silly buggers!').

I finally reached the road where there were about four cars parked, but not ours. I waited for a while, then decided to slowly start the walk back to Dundonnell.

After another half an hour she finally appeared in the car in the opposite direction having just come up from Dundonnell where she had returned and changed her clothing after a wet day out in Ullapool.

When I asked if she had been up the path about an hour ago, the reply was that she had only been back a short time, enough only to change (at Dundonnell) and come out to meet me.

The clothes that my wife was now wearing that evening were entirely different to what she was wearing in the morning when I last saw her. (She had, in fact, borrowed some clothes as she had got completely drenched in Ullapool.)

How would I have known that she was to change? The original plan was she would meet me on the A832 Dundonnell Road on her return from Ullapool, presumably in the same clothes when I last saw her in the morning.

How was it that I saw a mirage of her *in exactly the same clothes she had borrowed?* I could not have possibly been aware of that? A slight premonition, or just a somewhat bizarre occurrence?

But it is not only people who appear and then vanish. Buildings can, apparently, do that as well. Alan Boath, of Perth Road, Dundee, a very early member of *The Scotsman* mountaineering club (later renamed the Ptarmigan Club) told me:

Personally, I have had several unexplained and thought-provoking experiences over the years, both here in our own Scottish hills and also in the Lake District. These I have always attributed to fatigue as the majority have occurred during a hard day or weekend when I have been pushing myself.

However, the following did happen to a friend, three years ago, after we had been forced by bad weather to descend the cliff above Lochan nan Cat on Ben Lawers. During the long pad from the lochan to the road, I was well ahead so decided to wait for him to catch up.

When he did, he asked the name of the lodge we'd passed about a mile back. I told him there was no lodge on this side of Ben Lawers, but he persisted, so I got the map out and showed him. Again he was adamant and went on to describe the building in detail, right down to the blue and white curtains at the windows.

A couple of weeks later, he told his story to a mutual friend in the Tayside Police Mountain Rescue Team, adding how I'd tried to trick him.

When told yet again that there was no lodge in the vicinity of the lochan, he became so agitated that we had to change the subject. Even to this day he is still convinced that he saw a Victorian lodge on Ben Lawers.

But mistakes can be made. Take the case of the ghostly Highlander.

A kilted hillwalker with bloodied legs covered in scratches and midge bites, long hair, stockings around the ankles, shirt open to the waist, chest also covered in bloody bites and carrying a stick was descending to the roadside at Kintail.

There was intermittent mist. In a brief clear spell he saw below him a group of people standing beside a car. Also below him and above some steep outcrops of rock were three girls standing on a knoll and looking lost. A path or steep track ran near them down to the road close to the cars but they behaved as if they had not seen that.

In a gap in the swirling mist one of the girls looked up and the kilted hillwalker pointed his walking-stick in the direction of the track, indicating that was their best descent route. Then the mist came in again.

He didn't want to get caught up chatting, but later he saw the car group and the girls safely united by the roadside.

A year later he was in the dining car of a train from Fort William when he heard a party of American girls talking.

They were excitedly telling one another of a girlfriend who had Scottish ancestry and who had come to Scotland to research her ancestors. This girl and companions had got temporarily lost in Kintail and one of them had hurt an ankle.

Then, to their friend's astonishment, the mist had parted and a kilted spectral figure with bloodstained legs, a torn bloodied shirt, carrying a sword had pointed down to where a path led to safety and then the mist had closed in again! They had never seen him again, but he (they said) was probably a ghostly ancestor.

CHAPTER TWENTY-FIVE

DEVIL OF A TIME

The cause of the witchcraft and devil worship persecution which swept Scotland in the sixteenth and seventeenth centuries also affected nearly every country in Europe, but witches and warlocks were pursued with a ferocity in Scotland which was unknown in many other lands.

It inevitably had a place in naming sites within the landscape. Any dark grotto, deep pool, cavern or ravine tended to be named after the devil or to be associated with witches or evil in some fashion.

There are any number of Devil's Lochs sprinkled around the hills and yet not all are in dark sites, but I can only think of one Paradise Pool, which is a modern name for a boyhood swimming-pool in the Wharry burn in the Ochils – and even that was described as the Deil's Bucket by some local people.

The devil's influence is all over the hills. Some of the Border hills were believed in legend to have been dropped by the devil who intended to fly much further north, but as he flew from England with English hills in his creel the carrier broke and gave us some of our best Southern Uplands hills.

The old military road from Altnafeadh, near the eastern entrance to Glen Coe, to modern Kinlochleven and part of the West Highland Way, was called the Devil's Staircase, but that may have been because so many Highlanders hated the 'new road' as a threat to their way of life. The name pops up all over the place. The Devil's Kitchen above Loch Callater, near Braemar; the Devil's Elbow where the road from Glen Shee ran over to Braemar and which is now straightened out; the Devil's Beef Tub, near Moffat, in Dumfries and Galloway; the Devil's Loch on Dumyat, in the Ochils, and many more. Some gorges or pools called the Devil's Mill were named because the rumbling stones in the water continued to grind on the Sabbath.

The rocky wart of Clachnaben (589m, 1,900ft), which is so clearly seen from the Fettercairn to Banchory B974 road, one of these glorious fringe-of-the-Cairngorms hills, is also linked to the devil.

The hill's name comes from *Clach na Beinne* or Stone of the Hill. Its great, granite summit rock sticks up for 30m, but can easily be gained from the back. A local legend says that in the midst of a row with his wife, the Devil tore up the rock from a valley and flung it to the top of the hill where it crushed and killed her. Not far away is the Devil's Bite, a dry, rocky gap cut by glacial meltwater.

The Whangie, a prominent rock canyon on the eastern fringe of the Kilpatrick Hills, has devil associations. Sited south of Drymen and north of Milngavie and to the west of the A809, it is a well-known rock-climbing corner.

The name Whangie comes from the Scots for a split – it is a long, deep chasm on the north-west and west side of Auchineden Hill. It is 50 feet deep, the width varies from three to ten feet and its length is about 300 feet. The route through the chasm twists and turns: children love it.

The Devil is reputed to have met with witches and warlocks on the Campsies and was on his way to another conference at Dumbarton when, as he was flying over Cameron Muir, he whisked his tail and this made the cleft. Geologists say the action of ice created it (very unexciting).

There are not many heavenly names in our hills. The devil wins hands down. The so-called Angel's Peak in the Cairngorms is a relatively modern name which has wrongly replaced an older and far more attractive name, Sgor an Lochain Uaine, the Sharp Peak of the Green Lochan of Cairn Toul. The culprit was Alexander Copland, first chairman of the Cairngorm Club and an access activist, and why he renamed Sgor an Lochain Uaine is not clear.

It was probably intended as an antidote to Devil's Point, that rocky peak which dominates the eastern end of the Lairig Ghru and which links in an exhilarating ridge with Cairn Toul.

The name Devil's Point is a polite euphemism. The Gaelic name for Devil's Point is *Bod an Deamhain* (pronounced pote an dyaw-in) which means the devil's penis. Some authorities say it looks very wrinkled; others that the devil had two sexual organs and from certain angles the hill looks like that.

CHAPTER TWENTY-SIX

THE VANISHING HUNTER

One of the main problems in analysing alleged psychic phenomena in the hills is that some people don't want to be laughed at.

A good friend, scientist and naturalist, who is now retired from a Government agency, told me – amid assurances of good faith – that he and a fellow naturalist had encountered a strange man in the Kirkton Pass, which links Balquhidder (pronounced Balwhidder) with Glen Dochart, in Perthshire. He gave me permission to use their experience, but no names were to be mentioned.

The Kirkton Glen takes its name from the old church at Balquhidder, known to the clans of the glen, Stewarts, MacLarens, MacGregors and Fergussons. Rob Roy MacGregor, cattle dealer, warrior-chief and folk hero (1671–1734), is buried outside its ruined walls. Just behind the ruined church and its neighbouring nineteenth-century 'modern' church, is a large crag, Creag an Tuirc, Crag of the Boar, which was the Clan MacLaren gathering ground. It is also known as the Manse Crag. There is a cairn to the clan on its summit. Balquhidder Glen is a lovely place, beloved of the literati of past times.

The Kirkton Pass runs due north up the now conifer-wooded Kirkton Glen and rises steeply to a prominent crag called Creag an Eireannaich, sometimes given as Crag of the Irishman, but which is probably 'of the goat's leap'.

There is a tiny lochan at the crest, much visited by anglers and large char have been caught there. The path then descends more gently over rough moorland to the farm at Ledcharrie and the main A84 Lochearnhead to Crianlarich road.

It is a former cattle drovers' route and has known the tramp of warring clansmen as it is an obvious through-pass north and south. Some drovers used it to dodge tolls on the roads. The ground on the south side is owned by the Forestry Commission and the pass has legal right-of-way status.

The two naturalist-scientists were doing a bird count and were descending from the top of Creag an Eireannaich when they saw a man in old-fashioned clothing, carrying what looked like an ancient musket or fowling piece and accompanied by two deer-hounds.

The deer-hounds particularly caught their eye as they are graceful animals and because deer hunting with dogs is nowadays banned by law. They thought he might have been poaching. Dogs were used in the days of arrows and chancy firearms to pull down wounded deer.

They took different routes off the crag to accost him at the bottom, but when they got there he had vanished.

The base of the crag has many large boulders and they cast around these, hoping to see the man and his dogs, but to no avail. They were truly astonished not to find him.

They wrote a formal report for their organisation and they made exhaustive enquiries of the Forestry Commission and local people about the man and his deer-hounds, but without success.

They were puzzled by this because in a well-farmed and popular glen like Balquhidder, the dogs, in particular, would have been noticed.

I publicised this item in some outdoor magazines – but without names – and asked Balquhidder people about it in an attempt to get further information.

Then a Mr Donald Ferguson, of Dundas, New South Wales, Australia, wrote to me saying that he had seen my item about the Kirkton Glen figure in a magazine.

He wrote that it '. . . brings to mind a story I was told in 1927, when I was six years of age, by my grandfather, Donald Ferguson, born in 1852. His father, Donald, owned a farm at Kirkton in the early 1800s and I was told that my great-grandfather had seen 'phantom hunters and their deer-hounds passing through a local forest', so the story goes back at least to the mid-1800s.'

There were two follow-ups to this event. Mr Douglas N. Lowe, of Deanpark Avenue, Balerno, Midlothian, who is a tax inspector and a director of the Scottish Rights of Way Society, wrote to me on 30 September 1990, telling of an odd experience in the pass.

During 1979, whilst walking over from Balquhidder to Ledcharrie . . . the weather changed, where a constant cold brisk wind started up, laced with the odd sleety-feeling shower of rain (it was June).

As I reached the lower slopes, closer to the burn, I felt that we (my dog, Briagha, and I) should stop and have a bite to eat. I found a crater-like hollow, grassy/stony sides and about shoulder deep. I sat at the bottom of this hollow and poured myself a cuppa and started to dig out my eats.

I noticed that although out of the wind, which was cold enough, it was even colder *in* the hollow. It was bitterly cold, in fact. I remember zipping up my jacket and putting on my gloves.

I further noticed that the dog wasn't beside me. Usually by this time I would have expected the dog to have her head in my bag. She sat stoically on the lip of the hollow, hackles raised. She would not come down into the hollow even with the encouragement of a piece being offered to her.

She had also started a sort of whining growl. Thinking she must be hurt, I went up to check her out – no problem – and she bounded off showing that she wanted to go on.

I tried to 'help' her down into the hollow, but she wasn't having any of it. Descending back to my pack, I felt the cold was getting worse, quite unpleasant, in fact.

The dog was now lying at the lip of the hollow continuing her whining growl. Looking at her, I realised that she was staring past me as if at something else. There was nothing else in the hollow that I could see. I remember the hairs on the back of my neck rising at this. I packed quickly and continued on our way, much to the dog's obvious relief.

However, I didn't see anything, I didn't even sense anything, apart from the bitter cold, but obviously the dog did. My dog is never one to pass food by or even to pass a cosy bield away from the weather.

The bitter cold in the hollow I can't explain. Was it just caused by the wind whipping across the surface? Also, the cold seemed to intensify, or was that just me reacting unconsciously to the dog's unease. It didn't seem to affect the tea I had poured out as it was still piping hot when I returned it to my flask before heading off.

Douglas Lowe's anecdote brings up two points which occur a lot in stories of haunted bothies: a feeling of intense cold and the uneasy behaviour of dogs towards some unknown and unseen person or being – behaviour which catches the attention of the puzzled owner.

CHAPTER TWENTY-SEVEN

BUMPS, BANGS AND GROANS

It is a puzzle why so many incidents of spooks, groans, thumps and noises in the night are linked to bothies. These little cottages in the hills and glens are generally of no great antiquity and are mostly the result of the creation of the nineteenth-century big sheep farms and sporting estates.

Some are on the sites of older townships from the days of the clans and the old cattle economy and it can make some hillwalkers sad to look at a green corner in the bend of a river or burn or in a sheltered glen or strath and see the rushes and the bracken gradually reclaiming an area which once rang to the voices of young people and children.

The word bothy comes from the Gaelic *bothan*, meaning a small or makeshift dwelling. The buildings the hillwalker comes across today were either the homes of a shepherd and his family or a temporary dwelling for a deer watcher or stalker or an overnight shelter for shooting parties in the hey-day of Edwardian and Victorian deer-stalking. A handful were croft-farms.

A few are substantial buildings of two storeys, but most are low-slung with two rooms downstairs and a ladder-stair leading to sleeping quarters in the loft with the ruins of pens and a byre outside.

Many are in delectable spots and it is not surprising that when these buildings became empty they were used by mountaineers and hillwalkers as overnight refuges or as a base to climb hard-to-get-at hills. Changed agricultural practices, a reluctance of modern people to live in such isolated places and the development of estate vehicles all led to their demise.

They tend to be spartan inside, generally stone walls and a wooden or stone floor and a sleeping platform of wood upstairs, a fireplace and perhaps an old stone or log for a seat. They are unlocked. Some verge on the luxurious with woodlined walls and plenty of firewood in a nearby wood.

The mentioning of a bothy by name does not mean that it is still open to the public as an unlocked shelter because within the past year some bothies have been closed.

It was always a glorious feeling to head off into the hills with food and gear for several days, to carry a heavy pack many miles across a broken or winding path; to cross moors, to wade burns and then to tramp round a bend in a glen and see a mile or so ahead the roof of the bothy.

It was a great feeling to push open the door and dump the pack and then wander through the rooms and upstairs and sense the old familiar feeling of 'home' – the small, dust-covered windows and sills trapping many flies, rows of empty bottles on the mantelpiece or window sill with the remnants of candles sticking out of them; spare, tinned food left for the next hill gangrel; a battered logbook whose entries could provide happy reading (or at least it could until very recent times when to draw pictures of male genitals and write obscenities passes as being sophisticated and clever).

It was good, too, to set up one's stove on the table or on a window sill or floor and cook a meal. Then to settle down in front of a fire with the light of the flames or candles flickering on the walls, while outside one could hear the chuckle or rumble of the burns, the sound of rain on the roof or the wind fingering its way round the walls and roof, looking for chinks.

Two factors which affect the supernatural come together in the bothies. The first and mystifying one is that most are *not* old. The second is that they are undoubtedly home, albeit temporarily, for people and families. Their memories, thoughts, hopes, fears; their days of happiness or sorrow, are all part of the bothy's pedigree – sometimes so marked that it can often be clearly felt by all but the most insensitive.

It also has to be emphasised that most people using the bothies are outdoor people and not easily given to thinking of ghosts and spectres. They are accustomed to the sounds, scents and sights of the wild. They are aware that deer sometimes rub against bothy walls, that rats and mice make their homes in the walls or under the floor, that hooded crows or other birds sometimes land on the roof and make scraping noises or thumps, that the scream of the vixen can sound so much like a human voice that it sets the hair on end, and that the wind can blow through crannies and make groaning noises and almost heave sighs.

When I stayed at the old farmhouse at Carnmore, near the Fionn Loch, in that wild and glorious corner of the Letterewe estate, to the north-west of Loch Maree in Wester Ross – which is privately owned and not an open bothy – I was told that other visitors were convinced they had experienced a ghost because they heard rumblings and scrapings and could not immediately trace its source. It later turned out to be a badger which had got underneath the floorboards.

One must be on guard, too, for pranks. Glen Lichd bothy, in Kintail, which is in the care of St Andrews University Mountaineering Club, was reputed to be haunted – and perhaps it is – but one student told me that he and friends had spread a this-place-is-haunted rumour just for the fun of it. Another student told me of a girl in their group making tea for everyone and she kept making an extra cup as if some additional person was present. This was the subject of jokes and banter until it kept on happening and made them all uneasy.

Some tales grow in the telling. The best known is Ben Alder bothy, a former shepherd's and stalker's cottage, on the shores of Loch Ericht, and not far from the area where the famous Cluny's Cage was sited. It was a refuge shelter erected by the Clan MacPherson as one of the 'safe houses' for their fugitive chief, Cluny MacPherson, who stayed for five years on his clan lands after the 1745 Jacobite Rising failed.

It is frequently said that Ben Alder cottage has a spectre, the ghost of a stalker called McCook who allegedly hanged himself there. This tale is *not* true and has been denied by his family and with chapter and verse.

W.H. Murray, whose outdoor writings now have classic significance, has some significant things to say about Ben Alder cottage.

Bill's two main books, *Mountaineering in Scotland* and *Undiscovered Scotland*, were first published in 1947 and 1951, and were happily reissued in modern times. He now lives on the fringe of Lochgoilhead, in Argyll.

There is possibly no other mountaineer in Scotland who is held in such respect. He was one of a small group who led the renaissance of severe Scottish winter climbing in 1935–49. Captured in North Africa during the

Second World War, he wrote *Mountaineering in Scotland* in prison camps. The draft was seized by the Gestapo. The second draft was written in Czechoslovakia (now the Czech Republic) and Germany. *Undiscovered Scotland* followed.

He was a founder member of the Alpine Climbing Group, president of the Scottish Mountaineering Club, and the deputy leader of the Everest reconaissance expedition which prised open the door for Lord Hunt's successful expedition. Bill is a noted conservationist, the author of the definitive book on Rob Roy MacGregor (plus other books on outdoor and travel subjects), holder of the Royal Scottish Geographical Society's Mungo Park medal and an O.B.E.

Bill Murray says of tales of spectres and ghosts: 'It is the usual weakness of these tales that one never meets the first-hand witness.'

Then he did.

Bill was told by Robert Grieve (later Sir Robert, chairman of the former Highlands and Islands Development Board and a Glasgow University professor), a fellow member of the Scottish Mountaineering Club, that he and a friend had spent a most disturbed night in the cottage.

Bill writes:

They were having an after-supper pipe in their sleeping bags when they heard footsteps entering the room next door and tramping noisily on the wooden floor. In a short while they rose and went next door to investigate, but to their astonishment found no one there.

They returned to bed. The footsteps recurred, not indoors this time, but outside on the cobbled causeway, which runs against the front wall.

The noise was that of heavy, nailed boots on the stone, pacing back and forth, up and down the front of the cottage, and this was accompanied by brief pauses when Grieve and his companion strongly sensed that they were being watched from the window.

They had the additional feeling of being regarded with hostility as intruders. That drove them into the open with electric torches, but as before nothing was to be seen, They inspected the outhouse and barn with the same result, and there was no other cover. Again they retired to bed. And again footsteps entered the room next door.

After some aimless tramping there came a moment's pause, then the quite distinctive sound of heavy furniture being dragged over the floor, the kind of noise that would be made by the legs of a heavy table.

Grieve and his friends were well aware that there was no furniture next door [there was in the future], so they once more went through to look and found – a bare and empty room. They gave up then and retired for the night. Grieve freely affirms that he now felt frightened. But apart from continued noises no untoward event occurred.

That, of course, is by no means the only report of the hauntings, but it is the only report I can trust. Grieve is a level-headed and practical man. He does not go around telling this story, for he feels that normally other men discredit abnormal experiences in which they themselves had no share, and their disbelief confounds the man who knows his experience to be true, yet not so important to the world as to be worth exposing to ridicule. Grieve, in short, convinced me as a reliable witness.

However, a number of hill trampers have reported odd happenings at this bothy. They include a friend of mine, Nigel Hawkins, mountaineer, public relations expert, director and founder-member of the John Muir Trust and a former Council member of the National Trust for Scotland, who was also unnerved by rustlings and banging noises sounding like furniture being dragged across the floor. This would be hard to do now because the last time I was there all the furniture had either been removed or burned by vandals. Nigel ended up sleeping outside.

Professor Norman Collie, one of the giants of Scottish and world mountaineering, is reputed to have heard 'noises' in Ben Alder bothy, but tale-tellers may have confused this unsubstantiated episode with Collie's role in the stories of the spectre popularly called the Big Grey Man of Ben MacDhui (see page 19).

Mr Gordon Stewart, of Gargunnock, near Stirling, kindly loaned me some papers belonging to a Mrs Margaret Quinlan, a keen hosteller and hill tramper, who died in New Zealand on 15 August 1988, aged 85. Mr Stewart knew Mrs Quinlan for many years before her marriage – her maiden name was Davie Henry. She was usually known as Meg.

She told of going to Ben Alder bothy with friends where they met two English lads there working with the Ordnance Survey who had been there for ten days.

They said they had been disturbed by knockings on the walls and had heard the movement of a horse in a shed next to the bothy.

Mrs Quinlan, who in later years became blind, dictated some of her memories of the Scottish hills to a New Zealand friend, and she wrote of an earlier visit to the bothy in June 1945 when she was accompanied by a friend, Elizabeth Stewart.

She wrote that an old friend, Andy Tait, then chief-gamekeeper on Sir John Stirling Maxwell's Corrour estate, had tried in vain to prevent her going to the bothy because ghostly voices had been heard and he thought the two women might be alarmed.

She records:

We entered the front room in which was a plain wooden table, some big stones to sit on, plenty of cut wood to make a fire and in the cupboard tinned food which would only be used in emergency by someone who had no food with them.

Elizabeth was a dab at making a fire. She sat on one of the big stones. She sliced up wood and before long had a gorgeous fire alight. We cooked up a meal and then wondered what to do with ourselves.

Elizabeth was sitting on her big stone, with her axe in her hand ready to cut some more wood – a branch which was across her knee, when all of a sudden we heard voices – two people speaking. Elizabeth sat like a statue.

I got up to my feet and went out to the door to look in the three directions from which people could come. Nobody to be seen – only the voices! Back I went into the cottage.

Elizabeth was still sitting like a statue. She hadn't moved. She said 'What is it? I can't see anybody.' It was an eerie experience and I daren't have let Elizabeth know that I was feeling a bit frightened, so I thought it was time we retired for the night. I suggested we collect all the stuff and go into the little room at the back.

This we did and I locked the door.

I was just about asleep when outside the window of the little room, I heard two people speaking again and Elizabeth's voice said 'Meg, are you awake?' and I knew I daren't sympathise.

I feigned that I had not heard her speak and that I was sleeping. I lay for quite a long time unable to sleep, but gradually the room lightened and I thought of the old saying 'Ghosts march at midnight' and midnight must be past.

Next morning we both awoke fairly early and got up. Elizabeth lit the fire and we cooked a good breakfast. Then we left the cottage tidy and set out for our tramp back to Loch Ossian hostel.

As we were making our way down through the bogs we started to talk and Elizabeth confided to me that she was a terrible coward and her mother said she wasn't to go to such a place, but Elizabeth told her that I, Meg, was used to sleeping in such places and had no fear.

No fear? I had been so scared that when I heard the voices, I couldn't sit still but had to go out and explore to find out where the voices came from.

Then I admitted to Elizabeth that I had heard her speak to me during the night, but I knew that we couldn't cross to civilisation in the dark so I feigned that I was asleep. We said that one day we would return to the cottage, but not alone.

The following Saturday in the bus station in Glasgow, while I was waiting for a bus to Balloch, I met some of my old pals, members of the Lomond Mountaineering Club. They asked me where I was going.

I said Loch Lomond Hostel and they scoffed at me and said I was getting to be a softie.

But when I informed them that Elizabeth Stewart and myself had spent a night the previous week in Ben Alder cottage, they immediately asked if we had heard the voices and their estimation of me went sky-high. They, too, had heard the voices and they had done everything possible to try and find out the cause, but they could not.

Syd Scroggie, that marvellous mountain man of great courage, told me of an extraordinary event in Ben Alder cottage.

As part of a BBC radio programme he told me of an incident in the bothy when accompanied by two friends, Frank Anderson and Danny Fagan. An incident which he described as being like the activities of a poltergeist.

We were redding up the bothy preparatory to leaving one morning. There was a howling wind outside, lashing rain and dense mist. I took out of my rucksack a packet of biscuits – an unopened packet of digestives – and I put them on the mantelpiece of the bothy and said, 'We'll just leave these here for the gods of the bothy.'

Frank and Danny looked up and as they did so the packet of biscuits lifted itself off the mantelpiece, hovered just under the ceiling, moved right across the room, down the other wall and landed on the far side of the room, standing on end.

Well, that would have been explained at one time by the existence of a mischievous spirit lurking around in the bothy, but I don't believe that! I know perfectly well that the force that moved that packet of biscuits, lifted it up, moved it across and landed it with such apologetic delicacy at the far end of the room, that force came from Danny Fagan.

He didn't know he was exercising the force. He didn't know he was doing it. It was all done on the subconscious level and I think I know why he did it.

We'd had a rough time getting to the bothy in black dark. Me, the older guy, him the younger and slightly rebellious, you know. 'That blind so-and-so Scroggie, he's put me through all this to get to this bothy.'

Next day, when I put that packet on the mantelpiece Danny subconsciously said, 'He is putting that there. I'm going to frustrate his intention.'

You see, without knowing he was doing it. Lifting it up across the room, down the other side. Now, he could have lowered those biscuits so fast that they would smash to pieces and that would satisfy his own vents against this blind fellow Scroggie, but no, there was a hint of apology at the end.

He landed them so delicately that no biscuit was damaged.

I said to Syd that the cynics of this world might say on hearing this Ben Alder anecdote that the three men should have put more water into their dram.

Syd replied, 'We'd finished that the night before. It was only a miserable quarter bottle, anyway! However, that's explicable in my terms at any rate.'

Syd went on to tell of another experience:

This one I can't explain. Danny and I had an arduous journey, benighted half the time. Neither of us had been to bed in the cottage before. However, we got there.

We went inside and got a candle going. We sat down in one of the rooms and shut the door. Then we got the stove going and we had something to drink and we had a dram.

We had a quarter bottle of Dewars and then we turned off the stove (and, as everybody knows who has been in a bothy before, when you turn off the stove silence comes in under the door).

We were just sitting there when behind me on the door there came tappings, rapid tappings. The idea you got in your head was it was a hand or hands with big horny fingernails, tapping, tapping, tapping. Sometimes high up on the door and sometimes low down.

That stopped and then we heard, tramp, tramp, tramp from the neighbouring room. Great big, hobnail boots tramping up and down on the floorboards and then we heard noises which could only be described as furniture being moved around.

Not little delicate Sheraton tables, but what sounded like great big sideboards and grand pianos moving around on the bare boards, shuddering and shrieking across the floorboards and then a series of long agonised human groans!

I can't explain that one. I don't think Danny was responsible for that one, subconsciously!

I put it to Syd that in telling such an anecdote he was laying himself open to ridicule – people would say he must have imagined it or that it was auto-suggestion in some way. He stuck by his story and replied, 'Well, I might conceive of one person imagining something, but not two people imagining the same thing at the same time.'

Mr John Blair, of Polton Bank, Lasswade, Midlothian, a member of the Highways Hillwalking Club, wrote to me in February 1990 to tell of an incident at Ben Alder cottage in April 1982 when he was accompanied by a friend, Ian Strachan.

John wrote that they had been at Culra (pronounced cul-ray) bothy the previous night, a bothy which lies on the north side of Ben Alder.

Ben Alder cottage then had an iron bed. John says:

I got the iron bedstead, since we'd been at Culra the previous night. There were five others there and I'd lost the toss for the sixth place on the platform. So at Ben Alder we were on our own, and Ian slept on the floor by the bed. I had a Karrimat on top of the springs.

I lay and dozed as the fire crackled and burned itself out. Eventually, it became so dark inside the bothy that there was only blackness in the fireplace. Then it was possible to make out the small rectangle of window.

As I dozed, there was a terrific crash and the fire burst back into life, with the shadows of our socks and things dancing on the ceiling. I sat bolt upright and said 'Jesus Christ!' out loud. Ian was asleep, however, and heard nothing.

I lay for a while longer, eventually tiring and dozing.

Suddenly, the bedsprings near my head began a very regular plunking sound. I even stopped breathing to see whether I was causing it myself but it came on for a minute or two.

I've only told one or two people about this as (you probably know) they start by assuming you're mistaken and try to explain it, but of course, they were not there!

At no time did I feel in any danger so I did not run out of the bothy as people apparently have done. It was something frightening in that I couldn't explain it, but not totally evil.

I did not mention any of this to Ian, though he had his own adventures. He awoke with a pain in his back, but he had rolled on to his ice-axe. When he raised his hand, he thought he was in a cage. He had rolled under the bed!

This was well after I fell asleep, probably about 3 a.m.!

Though I did not tell Ian, we ended up on the train next to a Glasgow girl and her mother. When we mentioned Ben Alder cottage, the girl said, 'Oh, that's where the bedsprings play a tune!'

Also, Ian later spoke to a female teacher at his school. She maintains that the same thing happened with the fire when she was at Ben Alder, though they hadn't even used it at all!

Mr Alan Cray, of Brownberrie Lane, Horsfourth, Leeds, wrote to me in December 1990, to say that he had heard footsteps in the cottage.

By 1976 I had established myself as an émigré Scots engineer in Leeds and put down roots in bricks and mortar. To help pay for the mortgage, two bachelor friends were living in my house.

One of them, Colin, was a keen potholer and mountaineer like myself and had spent several years in Aberdeen as a student.

One winter evening we were sitting talking after a pleasant day's walking in the Yorkshire Dales and the subject of the bothies in Scotland became the topic.

I told him the tale of when my then girlfriend, Anne, and I had walked across the moor in January 1966 to the cottage on a fine breezy day, arriving about 4.30 p.m. We gathered enough bogwood for a reasonable fire for the whole night, had a meal and a romantic moonlight stroll before retiring to bed in the room nearest the loch. It was a still night.

At about 2 a.m., the front door crashed open and I heard the sound of heavy footsteps walking into the other large room and then complete silence.

I got up (Anne slept like a log), went to the front door and found it closed. Then I searched the other two rooms in the bothy. I found no one or any sign of a visit and concluded I had been dreaming. The rest of the night was peaceful.

I consider myself fortunate that I had not heard the story of hauntings of Ben Alder cottage before that visit else I would have fled in terror.

My experience before and after of the supernatural has been nil and I am a rather sceptical person when it comes to tales of the supernatural.

CHAPTER TWENTY-EIGHT

CREAKS, THUMPS AND THUDS

Mr Iain Leggatt, of Broadlands, Carnoustie, in Angus, wrote to me in July 1990 to say that on 23 September 1980, he had encountered a 'presence' in a bothy not far from Lochnagar.

It was only a single-room structure built originally for shepherds and, when empty, provided a refuge for hillwalkers.

The front (and only) door fits as securely into the doorframe as any that are erected today – and perhaps better than most.

There is not a tree for miles, little loose rock and no track. The walls of the cottage are two feet thick and well cemented, and the roof strongly made with thick wooden beams and rafters and stout 'tiles' (or slates) atop.

I decided that I would aim to celebrate my 42nd birthday (27 September 1980) by sleeping inside the bothy for one night. I boiled up some water on my camping-gas stove, mixed an Oxo drink and ate rather too well of my packed meal – cheese and onion sandwiches.

Too early to sleep, I lit a candle and read on that chilly, cloudy night from the comfort of my sleeping bag until, I suppose, about an inch and a half of the candle had burned away. I then snuffed it out and switched over to my electric torch. At around 10 p.m. I decided to sleep so switched my torch off.

The floor was cold and hard — I was aware of it even through my travel rug, sleeping bag, li-lo and poncho — and so I was restless, shifting positions and speculating on the lives and times of the previous, early occupants of the bothy.

With a creeping sense of horror I realised that while my restless mind had been wrestling with these questions, I had been unaware of another presence in the bothy, but suddenly I could feel unmistakable pressures, as of animal paws, one on each of my ankles, one on each of my thighs.

Worse, I could now clearly hear subdued and threatening, 'Grrrrrrrr-grrrrrrrrr', but could only sense bared teeth and imagine drooling salivating jaws.

I was shocked into cold, breathless immobility, cowering into my sleeping bag. Gradually, I gathered my senses, controlled my breathing, clenched my fists (and jaws) and tensed the muscles in my body and legs. With a great shout, I suddenly arched myself upwards and forwards, kicking up violently with my whole legs, lashing out with my fists.

From a sitting position, still mostly enclosed by my sleeping bag, I peered through fearful eyes into the gloom of the building, but there was nothing to see except the sparse furniture. The door was securely shut.

It was one a.m. I tried to bring my breathing back under control but it was a long time before I managed it. Curse those cheese and onion sandwiches! Nightmares at my age!

I took hold of myself and lay down again. I slept fitfully and eventually raised myself at first light on Sunday morning.

After sweeping the floor and placing all my belongings in my rucksack, I came to the sleeping bag. I fastened the toggle-and-loop at the feet end. Thirty inches along the sleeping bag, again, one on each side, smudgy marks, as of dried mud – without doubt from an animal's paws.

My departure was more hurried than graceful . . .

There was to be a sequel to this event. For around 20 months, between 1979 and 1981, Iain Leggatt was an occasional volunteer helper at Camus House – Tayside Region's home for the elderly in Carnoustie.

Some months after my experience I was in conversation with a resident whom we called Auld Nairn. He had been a police constable serving several rural communities in Angus and was well steeped in the folklore of Angus and Mearns.

He knew I did a lot of hillwalking and asked me if I had ever come across, during my travels, a supernatural canine called the 'Hound of Mark'.

I gave my account of what I had thought I had experienced and he replied: 'Aye, ye've met the Hound of Mark then!'

Odd tappings in another bothy, Corryhully, on the fringe of Lochaber at Easter 1988 were reported to me in March 1991 by Mr Neil Clough, of Brownhill Lane, Holmbridge, Huddersfield. He read comments in a bothy logbook about ghosts and then heard loud banging and tapping near his feet, close to the fireplace.

'The noise was like a walking-stick tapping on the wall or floor and moved along the bothy tapping every five yards . . . this experience occurred four times.' A friend with Neil Clough heard nothing.

Neil speculated that static electricity might have something to do with it all – he wore a vest which crackled with it.

'All the same, it was frightening,' he says. 'If you can enlighten me, please do.'

In the old Abyssinia bothy – now collapsed – in Glen Kinglas, between Arrochar and Inveraray in Argyll, shepherds told of being uneasy about some 'presence' being there with them.

(The name Abyssinia derives from a local man, Iain Mór (Big John) who had served with the Army last century in what is now called Ethiopia. The ruler jailed the British consul. A British expeditionary force deposed him and put a British nominee on the throne. Iain Mór talked so incessantly about being in Abyssinia that the name became attached to his house and it is now on Ordnance Survey sheets.)

Dogs inside the bothy were reported to stand up, hair on end, and face the one way. They sometimes refused to go into one room and this made the shepherds and friends uneasy.

Mr Tom Gilchrist, of Middleton Kerse, Menstrie, Clackmannanshire, a member of the Ochils Mountaineering Club and a hill gangrel of over 40 years experience, tells of visiting Abyssinia bothy when he was 16 . . . and getting a fright.

Tom says:

Turning up into Glen Kinglas, I decided to drum up (heat a drink) at the old unoccupied house called Abyssinia.

As I turned off the track and approached the door of the house, a strange feeling of fear and terror came over me and I took to my heels running terrified along the track for about three hundred yards before collapsing exhausted and shaking at the side of the road.

When I had calmed down, I got my stove and made myself a cup of tea. Feeling a lot better after my 'brew', I carried on and the rest of my hike that day went by with no more 'incidents'.

I never mentioned the Abyssinia incident to anyone until about two years ago (1988) when a letter appeared in the *Scots Magazine* from a lady who as a child had often visited the house when it was used during the lambing season or when the shepherds were gathering in the sheep.

The house then was not occupied and was only used to make a meal for the workers on these occasions.

The woman's dog would growl and its hair would stand on end and they would hear voices and movements in the rooms above the kitchen. It seems something terrible had happened in the house some years ago.

Some episodes involving dogs are capable of natural explanation. Syd Scroggie was told of an incident in a bothy when a dog refused to go into a room, but it turned out that the room was infested with ticks.

Captain Ronnie Leask, of Trinity Road, Edinburgh, a friend of mine of many years, a first-class mountaineer, master mariner, energetic historian and keen naturalist, says:

The strangest, unexplained occurrence I've had took place at Staoineag bothy (between upper Glen Nevis and Loch Treig). A friend of mine, Bill Sandilands, a chemist, and I had just bedded down when there was a very loud thumping from the stairs leading to the disused attic.

It was exactly like footsteps descending the stairs. We, of course, were soon bolt upright but an investigation failed to find any cause.

Perhaps – and it's a long shot which I really reject because of the loud footsteps – it was a rat jumping down each step and the empty bothy, particularly under the stair, acted as a sounding board and magnified the noise.

I *know* it wasn't that, though, but *what?*

CREAKS, THUMPS AND THUDS

An Edinburgh man, Grant E. Ritchie, of Hugh Miller Place, told me in January 1991 that he had a mysterious experience in the Western Highlands the previous summer.

> As part of a walk from Glenfinnan to Strathcarron, I descended down the path to Maol Buidhe bothy in the gloaming of 6 July. I was disappointed to see a candle in the window.
>
> I prefer being alone and the prospect of company did not appeal. As I drew closer I could see that shimmering distortion above the chimney which indicates that hot air is rising.
>
> The bothy was empty. No candle, no fire!
>
> I had been walking for 11 hours having left Camban (a bothy in Glen Affric) in the morning. Perhaps exhaustion caused this hallucination?

David Trainer is an outstanding mountains man. He is a Roman Catholic priest of the archdiocese of Glasgow and has climbed in the Himalayas, the Alps and in North America, and made a study of the spirituality of mountain peoples. He is also a superb musician. He has raised thousands of pounds for charities and other good causes by undertaking sponsored treks of a historical or literary kind.

Father Trainer is known to his friends as Big Davy. He told me:

> In the middle seventies long distance backpacking was just becoming fashionable and with the introduction of all sorts of new equipment, lightweight tents and the like, it was also much more comfortable.
>
> I left my car in Braemar at a friend's house and set off across the Southern Cairngorm mountains. It was mid October. Five solitary days later I had moved from Lochnagar across to Glen Tilt and Glen Feshie, ending in the Corrour Bothy below Devil's Point and Cairn Toul in the Lairig Ghru. I decided to stay there in its spacious single room which was less cramped than the lightweight tent.
>
> As I was cooking my evening meal inside the bothy, I first of all felt the presence of what I thought was another hill climber. Then I heard footsteps – the clear sound of boots on the ground approaching the bothy. I was feeling quite excited about speaking to another human being after five days and I shouted out a greeting and something about the door being open.

Nothing happened. I went to the door expectantly and looked out. No one was there. Walking all the way round the bothy I could see no one in sight.

I began to feel a shiver of fear and panic. What is it the psychologists say about fight or flight? Well, I couldn't fight so I grabbed the map and made a few hurried calculations.

It was getting dark and Linn o' Dee (and the nearest road-end) was too far away for me to reach it before nightfall and my headlamp's battery was running very low.

I was still tempted to take a chance and go, but common sense got the better of me and I decided to stay. Later on in the night the footsteps came up to the door again but this time I didn't shout out. I was tucked up cringing in my sleeping bag cuddling my ice-axe!

In the morning I laughed it off as auto-suggestion and told myself how silly one can be when one is all alone in the hills.

A couple of days later when I got back to Braemar I was staying in the chapel house guest-room when I picked up an old book about tales of Deeside. It was only then I discovered that other people had similar manifestations.

One of these was Affleck Gray, of Pitlochry, the author of *The Big Grey Man of Ben MacDhui*, who as a young man frequently stayed at Corrour.

He tells of hearing the bothy door opening and shutting. He called out a greeting, but no one was there. Affleck spent ages jumping up and down on the floor trying to get the door to open and shut of its own volition, but it stayed firmly shut. There was no wind and the door sneck or catch was firmly lodged.

John Starbuck, of Daleview Gardens, Egremont, in Cumbria, arrived at Sourlies bothy, on the fringe of Knoydart, after 'a hot, tiring day' in late summer 1982. The bothy was empty; the only sign of life being a rat in the rushes by a nearby burn. He cooked a meal, but could not finish it.

Remembering the rat, I put the lid tightly on the saucepan and put the lot outside on the ground about three feet away from the bothy door so that it would not entice the rat into the bothy.

In the middle of the night I was woken by the outside door rattling vigorously for a few seconds. It then stopped, but no one came in and I could hear no other sounds. There was no wind. I dozed for a few minutes only to be woken again by the same noise.

This time I got up, went to the door and shone a torch through the door window, but I could not see anything that could be responsible. I returned to bed, but was soon woken yet again by the same noise, this time accompanied by the metallic sounds of something tinkering with the saucepan. I got up again and went outside, but there was still nothing there.

I do not mind admitting that by this time I was getting quite nervous.

I decided to rig a trap. I found a plastic bucket which I perched upside-down and loaded with rocks, on two forked sticks over the saucepan. At least, if it was the rat I might catch it, satisfy myself what all the commotion was about and get a good night's sleep.

But then a rat couldn't rattle a door, could it? A sheep perhaps? But there were none about and they are vegetarians, aren't they?

Well, at last I had a peaceful sleep, but in the morning I found that the bucket and saucepan had not been disturbed and I could not see any animal tracks or footprints on the ground.

No such events had taken place when I had stayed at the bothy two nights earlier, when there had also been three other people present.

To this day I have been unable to convince myself of what was going on that night. I tell myself it must have been an animal of some description; but what animal large enough to move a door would otherwise be totally silent and leave no trace of its presence?

I am not saying that I believe in the supernatural. Being well educated in the natural sciences, I believe there is a rational explanation for everything. But I cannot deny the powerful effect that doubt, at the instant of the moment in such events, has on the mind.

Invermallie bothy, in Lochaber, has cropped up several times in the bumps-and-thumps category and one incident in May 1983 involved two men both known personally to me – outdoor writer Clive Tully, one of a group who, in 1993, had a very enjoyable time in Spitsbergen and the Lyngen

Alps, in Arctic Norway, and Roger Smith, a fellow founder-member of the Scottish Wild Land Group.

Clive Tully recalls that the ground was very wet. 'I remember trudging up to that beautifully inviting shelter with the prime thought of getting my boots and socks off, and collapsing in front of a cheerful fire with a steaming mug of tea . . .'

The two men went to bed early, spreading their sleeping bags on the wooden floor.

It was about four in the morning when a loud crash woke me – I much prefer surfacing from my slumbers gradually, drifting through various stages of semi-consciousness before coming round. The echoing thud, and the clumping noises which followed it took me from deep sleep to wide awake in an instant and I could feel my heart almost competing with the noise as it tried to readjust after the sudden shock.

'Are you awake?' I whispered nervously to Roger. 'Did you hear that?' The clumping sounded as though some very late arrivals had wandered into the bothy, and were crashing about in their boots, trying to find the best room. The only trouble was, Roger had bolted the door from the inside to stop the deer and sheep getting in. A muttered grunt from Roger indicated that he too had heard the intruder.

Roger took his torch, and tip-toed to the door of our room. 'Anybody there?' he called into the gloom. Not a sound. He disappeared into the darkness, and I could hear him creeping about the other rooms of the house.

Roger reappeared. He was puzzled at not having found a single clue. The door was still bolted, and there were a few deer moving about out-side – certainly no nocturnal backpackers in the house, no stray animals, and definitely no unearthly apparitions.

We never did fathom out those strange thumping noises. To me, they were, without doubt, footfalls on the wooden floorboards somewhere in that house.

Roger Smith recalls: 'There is no logical explanation. If you are like me, you don't look for one. I have long been convinced that people long since departed can leave impressions for us to pick up, either in sounds or pictures. Somehow, that night, we got "tuned in" to another time for a brief moment. It certainly made our trip special.'

Leslie Barrie, of Argyle Road, Saltcoats, in Ayrshire, also reports strange noises at Invermallie bothy on 30 January 1982. He and a friend, Iain Miller, bedded down in the upper, left-hand room. Leslie says:

> I awoke in the early hours of the morning intensely cold and heard a noise which I can best describe as sounding like sighing and weeping. It seemed to come from beyond the closed door of the room, definitely from *within* the bothy.
>
> Iain turned over in his sleeping bag and thinking that he too had awoken, I asked if he had also heard the strange noises. Iain said that he had not.
>
> I have to admit that I never really managed to get back to sleep afterwards; a combination of feeling cold, and listening for more noises. Needless to say, there were no more noises. I should add that I am a light sleeper.
>
> As dawn broke, I went outside to find a calm morning with the cloud level low down on the hills. There was little or no wind. In view of the weather I am convinced that the noises were not caused by the wind blowing through cracks/holes in the skylights or elsewhere.
>
> Iain suggested that a possible explanation would be that the fire we had lit in the downstairs room before we had gone to bed would have caused boards to expand and contract thus causing strange noises.
>
> I tend, however, to discount this theory as the noise, for the short time I heard it, was fairly constant.
>
> Also, I can recall lying awake listening carefully and when I questioned Iain if he, too, had heard it, the noise stopped. The peculiarity of the sounds and the fact that they stopped in the way they did makes me tend to dismiss the wind theory. However, in retrospect, the wind – although unlikely – is the only logical explanation I can reach.
>
> I have read of other accounts of supernatural happenings which are often preceded by a sense of coldness. I am sure that I awoke because of the fact that besides being a light sleeper it was indeed a cold night and I had an inferior sleeping bag.
>
> I like to think I am open-minded about such matters and would

not go so far as to say whether my experience . . . was definitely super-natural. Iain assured me that there must be some logical explanation as to the cause and I tend to agree with his judgement.

Nor are such events confined to the Highlands. Mr David Nisbet, of Hay Lodge Cottage, Peebles, tells in July 1990 of stopping for the night at Shiel of Castlemaddie, 'an abandoned herd's cot' in the Galloway hills.

> I was sound asleep this night (1950) when I awoke with a very strong feel-ing that someone's hand was grasping my hair and tugging at it.
>
> I was startled but not unduly upset by this and soon fell asleep again. After several days wandering I found my way to my brother-in-law's home at Muirdrochwood, by Dalry. He was the forestry ranger for this district and he had a bitch Springer who had whelped. She had four bitch pups and one dog pup. I bought the dog pup and he was to become my constant companion on the hills in due course.
>
> Some years later I was back at the Shiel and, noting that half the living-room was filled up to the ceiling with hay, I chose to lie down in a different spot to the previous time.
>
> During the night I was awakened by exactly the same train of circumstances; in addition, my dog let out a wail and crashed into the living-room door. I lit a candle and found him lying stunned and twitching on the floor.
>
> I have thought about this over the years and can find no explanation.

A mystifying bothy anecdote came from Brian Cullimore, of Carleton, Carlisle, who stayed with a friend in the Hutchison hut after doing an ice climb in Corrie Etchachan, in the Cairngorms in early December 1986. They were in their sleeping bags by 8 p.m.

> We had eaten and dozed off and were woken at 11 p.m. by a very strange feeling of uneasiness in us both.
>
> Alan, my companion, was certain that he had heard footsteps approaching the hut and we were anticipating the arrival of some more climbers.
>
> They never arrived and a quick look outside the door proved that

there was no one in sight. The sense of tension was still there and neither of us dared to switch off our headtorches for quite a while.

Eventually, Alan dozed off, only to wake again and seeing my sleeping form woke me up telling me he had seen a snake in the hut!

This sense of uneasiness and visual/audible hallucinations lasted about two hours then suddenly went away. We then both slept soundly until the following morning.

The two of us have spent many nights in various bothies together and yet never experienced this kind of hallucination before or since.

But of all the bothy tales two of the strangest involve the Old Bynack Lodge – now a ruin – in upper Glen Tilt, in Atholl.

One of the most dramatic episodes I have come across was to read an article in an outdoor magazine about the experiences recounted by a Mr John T. K. Barr which took place during a wet and windy week in July 1958.

He had been accompanied by a group of Scouts from Paisley. They had sheltered in Bynack Lodge during a storm, but mysterious 'movements' had caused them to abandon their shelter and to camp.

The group had intended to walk through Glen Tilt to Braemar and then cross the Lairig Ghru to Aviemore, taking a week to complete the trip. They had intended to camp in Glen Tilt but the ground was sodden with heavy rain and the ruins of Bynack Lodge seemed a good place to spend the night.

It had been a two-storey building, but most of the roof had gone and much of the southern end of the house had collapsed. The front door easily opened. The ground-floor room to the right of the small entrance hall was dry and gave shelter.

[This building is now entirely ruinous.]

The group soon had a fire blazing and cooked a meal on their stoves. The room had a low table facing the fireplace and a large black empty trunk against the back wall. In one of the shorter walls was a boarded-up window. The fireplace lay in the centre of the longer wall (the outside wall) and between it and a rear wall was an alcove with a small, shuttered window. Opposite the fire and above the low table was a shelf about six feet up, holding a couple of rusty tin cans.

The group were sitting drinking coffee and discussing sleeping arrangements when an empty bottle holding a candle toppled over on a small shelf above the fire. It was broken right through in an almost straight line about four inches above its base.

Then a rusty tin can bounced on the floor behind the group in the centre of the room. It could only have come from the high shelf above the table. Thinking some animal had dislodged it, the Scouts clambered up on to the table to investigate, but there was an inch of dust on the shelf and no tracks. There was, however, a clean-cut circle in the dust where the can had been and although this was ten inches from the edge of the shelf there was no other disturbance visible and the second can had not moved.

The group became uneasy and then, with a crash, the shutter on the small window beside the fire burst open inwards and clattered against the wall. That was enough for the group and they all made for the door. They camped some distance from the building. The next morning in bright sunshine they examined the lodge in detail, but could find no explanation for the events.

Twenty years later Mr Barr returned, but the weather was so foul that he and other Scouts turned back. However, the following Saturday, accompanied by a patrol leader and an adult leader, he set out to reach the lodge again from the northern, Glen Dee, side.

They found the building had collapsed further. The room had gone and both downstairs rooms were open to the sky. Most of the walls were still standing although in a ruinous state. The shelf, the table and trunk had all disappeared and the alcove window now gaped out to give a back view down the glen. Grass grew on the rubble-strewn floor of the room where the Scouts had sought shelter.

The mystery remains . . . what kind of poltergeist once inhabited old Bynack Lodge?

Tom Gilchrist's son, Tom, and his wife had a strange experience while doing a winter traverse in the Cairngorms. Their experience is doubly odd because it occurred in the Sinclair Memorial Hut, a modern building at the north end of the Lairig Ghru and which was later demolished because of litter and ground erosion.

Just as they were about to get into their sleeping bags and blow out the candle they heard footsteps crunching through the snow and getting louder as they approached the bothy.

Tom sat up to see who was arriving, but the sound of the footsteps stopped outside the door. Tom then got up and taking his torch opened the door and looked out. It was a clear starry night, but he saw nothing.

He went back to bed and was soon asleep. He awoke suddenly during the night and again heard the footsteps. This time he got up, put on his boots and went outside. He walked right round the hut but could find no footsteps in the snow.

The one experience I have had of the allegedly supernatural did not take place on a mountain, but in a building.

In 1993 I was loaned a cottage at Little Gruinard, between Poolewe and Ullapool, so that I could get a children's adventure novel finished.

I arrived at Little Gruinard on the Saturday night and I was alone in the cottage, reading in the large kitchen, when I heard a large thump upstairs. I thought nothing of it, but then minutes later came a second thump. I went upstairs to have a look, but there was no one around, all the windows were closed and the one door was firmly shut. Apart from thinking the noises sounded like someone kicking shoes off, I thought no more about it.

The next morning George MacKenzie, the friendly and helpful ghillie/manager at Little Gruinard, called in and after chatting for a time told me the cottage had a ghost.

Trying to be funny, I said, 'Does it sit down on a bed and kick its shoes off?'

He looked at me in surprise and said, 'Yes, it does sound like that. So you've heard it?'

I said that it was surely only birds on the roof, or pine martens, or the central heating going off and on and making the cottage creak, but George said that with few exceptions the noises occurred only at weekends. Several guests had heard them. Nearly everyone had said it was like the sound of shoes being kicked off. It was a benign ghost. None of the normal 'natural' explanations fitted because of the timing of the noises. It was believed the wife of an earlier owner of the estate had killed herself in the house or nearby.

I heard nothing for the rest of the week. In April 1995 I returned to the cottage again to do some more writing, and this time I was accompanied by my wife, Agnes.

We arrived on the Saturday and on the Sunday night I was half asleep when I heard a clear 'thump' from the area of the bedroom door. I got up, but the door was open and fastened back. Agnes had opened a little window in a recess which had the old, outer window still in place and secondary double-glazing inside. She later heard a bang and thought 'That's the window banged shut'. She got up and examined it and found it was indeed shut. She was puzzled by this because there was no *inside* draught in the cottage. She also heard a bang at the door of the bedroom.

In recalling all this, details are hazy because we were half-asleep and stumbling around in the half-dark. However, we both – independently – felt a sense of oppression and uneasiness and I recall being relieved later to see by my watch that it was past midnight and, presumably, the ghost would now cease its activities. I felt a real sense of relief.

We heard nothing strange for the rest of the week, but in telling George MacKenzie about it he mentioned that one of the visitors had a little dog and it had refused to go into the bathroom area and exhibited signs of fright.

Was our reaction auto-suggestion, tiredness brought on by a long journey, or imagination working overtime in the half-dark?

THE BLESSED CORRIES

Author Neil Munro (1934–1960) is best known for his Para Handy stories, the amusing tales of the puffer, *The Vital Spark* (accurately described as a sea-going lorry), its eccentric crew and their high jinks up and down the west coast, but he also wrote historical novels of great quality: *John Splendid, The New Road, Doom Castle* and *Gillian The Dreamer*.

In *John Splendid* he depicts the novel's hero, young Elrigmore, trying to get back to Inveraray after the great Campbell defeat by the Marquis of Montrose's army at Inverlochy in 1645. Elrigmore realises he will eventually get home safely and he muses on the beauties of his native Argyll.

In this sensitive piece of writing – worth a place in anthologies – Neil Munro argues that the hills contain sites which by their atmosphere capture and hold the spirit, heart and mind of the wanderer. He makes it plain that this experience is not confined to theorists, but to practical people like the shepherd or hunter.

It is an experience known to many modern hill stravaigers.

[A few of the words may need explanation for some modern readers: brock is a badger, foumart is a polecat, and the cannoch is bog cotton.]

I know corries in Argile that whisper silken to the winds with juicy grasses, corries where the deer love to prance deep in the cool dew, and the beasts of far-off woods come in bands at their seasons and together rejoice. I have seen the hunter in them and the shepherd too, coarse men in life and occupation, come sudden among the blowing rush and whispering reed, among the bog-flower and the cannoch, unheeding the moor-hen and the cailzie-cock rising or the stag of ten at pause, while they stood, passionate adventurers in a rapture of the mind, held as it were by the spirit of such places as they lay in a sloeberry bloom of haze, the spirit of old good songs, the baffling surmise of the piper and the bard.

To those corries of my native place will be coming in the yellow moon of brock and foumart – the beasts that dote on the autumn eves – the People of Quietness: have I not seen their lanthorns and heard their laughter in the night? – so that they must be blessed corries, so endowed since the days when the gods dwelt in them without tartan and spear in the years of the peace that had no beginning.